THE

CHRISTIAN

WORKING

MOTHER'S

HANDBOOK

The Christian

H A N D

JAYNE GARRISON

Working Mother's
BOOK

Tyndale
House
Publishers
Incorporated
Wheaton
Illinois

Front cover and interior illustrations by Sally Springer

First printing, May 1986
Library of Congress Catalog Card Number 85-52165
ISBN 0-8423-0258-1
Copyright © 1986 by Jayne Garrison
Printed in the United States of America

CONTENTS

INTRODUCTION

Doing It All

It was my first day at work. Standing in the doorway to my new office, I looked every bit the picture of a career woman on the rise. Brown velveteen blazer, tweed skirt, brown leather pumps, immaculate makeup, and finely groomed hair. Mother would have been proud. But that, perhaps, was the problem. Mother wasn't home cheering me on. . . . *I* was the mother. Back home were a five-year-old daughter and a medical student husband, each depending upon me to pay the monthly rent and put dinner on the table. Though I practiced the deep breathing our childbirth instructors assured us would work in any of life's major crises, I trembled with fear of the unknown.

In minutes I would begin my training as an advertising copywriter. That in itself was frightening enough—what if I couldn't measure up? But nagging at the back of my mind was an even more threatening thought. For in addition to learning the ins and outs of my new job, juggling the roles of wife, mother, and copywriter would require me to take stock and make use of the truly important things of life . . . to grow up and out in every direction . . . to give up the self-centered-ness of young adulthood . . . to replace shabby, short-lived trends with inner growth and satisfaction . . . *to make every minute count.*

I had just entered the working mother's wilderness.

From this point on, life was certain to test and try me in a thousand different ways. I wanted to turn and run back to my car sitting in the parking lot, but was stopped by a feeling of shame as I remembered how hard good jobs were to come by. So, I took one step forward and walked into the window-less room.

"Please, God," I cried out silently, "just don't make me do this alone. That's all I ask. If this is your desire for my life, be with me—help me find my way through the wilderness. And help me to do it well.

"Amen."

FROM MY JOURNAL

Job interview with the local newspaper. My appointment is with the managing editor. As I walk back toward his office I feel ridiculously simple. My string sample book is too heavy and cumbersome, my dress too frilly and feminine. I can't seem to make conversation and neither can he, so the whole thing is over in minutes. I leave knowing that it's the last I'll ever see of the place.

"But, God," I cry out in pain, "I really needed that job—don't you care?"

GAINING CAREER POWER:

ONE

Finding Your Niche

Probably one of the most discouraging times of my life was shortly after college graduation. I was a late bloomer and had earned my degree under considerable hardship. I wanted so badly to work in my chosen field. I needed so badly to work—period. And so I interviewed and interviewed and interviewed. But always it was the same story: "I'm sorry, we really like your style, but you see, with so many newspapers going out of business we can hire someone with fifteen years' experience. Why should we hire a beginner?"

In the meantime, I found myself developing an acute case of diminished self-respect. Nothing seemed to matter. When Olie and Heather left for school, I sat down in my disheveled living room and wept. I didn't clean house; I didn't cook; I didn't sew. Actually, I'm not sure what I did. Somehow the hours disappeared and suddenly it was time to fetch Heather from school. That was my day.

When I did try to analyze the situation my thoughts always arrived at the same place. God had been so good to me in the past—had I received my quota of blessings? Maybe God had given up on me—because I certainly didn't feel his presence, not even when praying, reading the Bible, or meditating.

One day I shared my feelings with a friend.

"Jayne," she said, "you're not being sensible. You're not separating your emotions from fact. The fact is, God is always there, but you're not always going to feel his presence with the same intensity. Moods and feelings change—don't ever base your faith in God on feelings!"

I left my friend with an invigorating sense of well-being. Throughout the next week I verbalized her statement whenever those thoughts of desertion crept in. "I don't feel your presence, God," I would say, "but I know you're there and I love you for it."

Speaking the words flooded me with new peace. Now I was ready to approach life from where I was—at home in suburbia, unemployed, and scared to death.

To make a long story short, I did find a job. It was with an advertising agency in Dallas. My boss was a Christian as well as a mother and homemaker like myself; my responsibilities—creativity plus. It was truly the job the Lord had been holding for me and I *was* grateful.

Nevertheless, job hunting is an excruciating physical and mental strain. To help minimize this stress, I've developed the following pointers.

SURVIVAL TACTICS FOR THE CHRISTIAN JOB HUNTER

Job hunting wins a prominent spot in the list of life's downers. But it's important to remember that no one and certainly not a future employer is drawn to a depressed, melancholy person. People want that which delights and cheers them. But how to present such a picture when it seems no one has any use for you? If only I knew. All I can truthfully say is that we have to try. And not just for the purpose of presenting a positive image to outsiders, but for the sake of our families as well. I firmly believe that a family's health hinges upon the woman's state of mind.

So, if job hunting is getting the best of us, perhaps the first thing we should do is reevaluate our goals. Are we seeking to glorify God or man through our career? Growing in Christ involves answering the serious question of what position the career is to occupy in our overall responsibilities and priorities. Once we come to an understanding that our primary ministry is to love God, we are ready to tackle the second phase of finding a job that will occupy the proper place in our lives.

Setting some long- and short-term goals is one very good way to "get through" a jobless phase. Short-term goals in this context refer to everyday priorities such as house-cleaning—things we know we've mastered. Long-term goals refer to filling empty hours with new adventures—Scripture memorization, cooking gourmet dinners, sewing a garment. Need some direction? Back-to-school programs offer instruction from business classes to art training. Study something that excites you or that will make you a better job candidate. (It could be an impressive thing to reveal during an interview.)

Also consider spending this "in between" time engaging in something the entire family will benefit from. Try experimenting with ethnic cooking—your children will fondly remember your unemployment as the time Mom cooked only Chinese food. Or perhaps this period offers the "gobs of time" you've been waiting for to refurbish your houseplant collection. Read up on new varieties, explore care tips—make those green leaves shine with good health.

Creative fulfillment might also be reached through the making of house gifts for Christmas. Hook a rug, crochet an afghan, or paint a masterpiece. Your gifts will be doubly cherished when that new job leaves you with little time for craft work.

And how about exercise? Free time can be very beneficial if it helps you become regular in physical activity. Try running, aerobic dance, or swimming. Exercise habits developed during this interval will continue to be an asset once you've landed a job.

Other good ways to spend your spare time while job hunting include writing letters or reading books. Read classics. Read the Scriptures. Write down your insights and share them with a friend.

If you're in a congregation of elderly folk, check with the pastor about visiting needs. You could also volunteer to send get-well notes to the sick or sit with someone on the hospital's critical list.

Whatever you do, talk to people around you. Find out what

they need and how they feel. This is no time to withdraw—
reaching out keeps us vibrant and alive.

GETTING THROUGH THE LEAN DAYS AHEAD

Of course, passing the time during one's unemployment isn't
always the main issue. For many women, making ends meet
with a reduced income is the primary concern. Financial
problems can be particularly worrisome when Mother is
solely or even equally responsible for keeping the family
financially afloat. If this is your current situation, we're about
to explore some ideas that are certain to make unemployment a little easier and less stressful.

When it comes right down to it, our life-style depends
heavily upon whether we have time or money. Few people
have both. When we're busy and always in a hurry, convenience products and services *are* important. We have the
shirts laundered at the cleaners, eat in restaurants, buy at
overpriced shops, use more gasoline, throw away old clothes,
and pay expensive repair bills. When time is more abundant
than money, however, we wash our own clothes, eat nutritious,
home-cooked meals, shop at stores offering greater savings,
conserve gasoline, mend worn clothing, and do most of our
own household maintenance. If you have quite suddenly
found yourself between jobs, the idea of sacrificing convenience during your unemployment phase may be frightening.
But once you stop to realize that you temporarily don't need
these "helpers," you'll be free to enjoy this period as a God-
given rest from the daily struggle of hurrying to and fro.

Here are some suggestions for getting through the days
ahead.

1. Surround yourself with people who aren't hung up on
    material success. You may find these friends in your
    church, a community drama society, or perhaps at the
    Y.M.C.A. runners' club. The point is to spend time culti-
    vating an activity that will expose you to people who are
    consumed with constructive interests rather than a finan-
    cial ego.
2. Get reacquainted with your sewing machine. With more

women working these days, I suspect I'm not the only one to have laid sewing aside during especially busy stages of life. However, when one is short of cash, sewing can be a lifesaver. Hunt for interesting fabrics at unlikely places such as discount stores. Keep styles simple—you may not be as skilled as you used to be. And keep your secret savings to yourself. Don't tell people that the fabric was only $1.50 a yard at the discount store, and especially keep it from your youngsters! Though you can share your resourcefulness later on when they're older, children are especially sensitive during hard times. Your handcrafted creations should be an image builder, not a source of anxiety.

3. Instead of buying books and magazines, make use of the library. After you get that new job, you may indeed be too busy to meet library hours. But for now, what better way to get something for nothing! While there, be sure to check your local newspaper for free concerts, seminars, and children's activities. Something as simple as a shopping mall's promotional petting zoo can become a sensational treat to children—if introduced as such.

4. If there are small children in the family, eat outdoors as often as possible. You'll find the fresh air relaxing, and your children will hardly notice the absence of expensive activities when there is something such as this to look forward to.

5. Rather than pay expensive hairdressing fees, have your hair groomed at a school of cosmetology. Though you probably won't get to ask for a particular hairdresser, you'll be in the hands of a graduating senior student—and for a fraction of what you'd pay at a regular salon.

6. Make it a habit to think conservatively. Learn to save money in hidden opportunities.

■ Save the cotton that comes in the top of a medicine bottle. It can be used for manicures or crafts.
■ Use half of a dryer sheet for softening fabrics in the dryer.
■ Cut paper napkins in half. (Cloth napkins are an even wiser option.)
■ Stretch your milk money by mixing equal parts of powdered and fresh milk.

7. Frequent resale shops, but think creatively. An oversized scarf could be made into an interesting top for your teenager. The Hawaiian dress in size large might have enough fabric in it for you to cut out your preferred style.
8. Replace expensive cleaning agents with products such as ammonia, bleach, and rubbing alcohol.

■ For cleaning floors, tile, woodwork, and shower stalls: mix 1/2 cup ammonia with a gallon of water.
■ For cleaning toilets and removing scuff marks or finger-prints: use ammonia full strength.
■ To clean and deodorize enamel, porcelain, glass, tile, marble, and woodwork: add 2 tablespoons of bleach to a quart of water. Wash surface, rinse well.
■ Make your own window spray by mixing rubbing alcohol and water.

9. Get the most mileage from your makeup.

■ Foundation will last longer if mixed with a small amount of moisturizer in the palm of your hand before applying. If your powder blush compact breaks, save the pieces in a jar, grind with a clean spoon, and apply with a brush.
■ Use inexpensive petroleum jelly as an economical mois-turizer, lip gloss, nail and cuticle conditioner.
■ Replace costly bath gels with this revitalizing shower mix: Combine 1/2 cup lime juice, 1/2 cup lemon juice, and 1 cup mineral water. Apply the mixture to your body with a clean sponge. Rinse off with clear water in the shower.
■ Remove makeup with vegetable shortening. Massage into skin and wipe excess off with tissue.

FEEDING THE KITTY

When unemployment extends over a long period of time, you may find it necessary to take a temporary job. This is par-ticularly true if one is searching for employment in a crowded field. In advertising, for example, it's quite common for writers, artists, and even account executives to fill in as agency "go-fors" during unemployment intervals. The flexibility of part-time hours and the understanding that the participant is looking for a more permanent position make such a job ideal for scheduling interviews and keeping track of new work opportunities. But if your area of work isn't conducive to this type of arrangement, there are still many other ways to earn money while you're seeking that perfect job.

Unless you're temporarily dropping out of the job market, it's important to remember that your job search remains of foremost importance. Don't get so ambitious with temporary money-raising projects that you miss out on longed-for opportunities. Nor should you bite off more than you can chew. All promised work should be completed on time even if a career job opening comes up.

There are lots of books on making money at home, but here are a few of my favorite ideas.

SELL A PRODUCT

Good Cheer Baskets. The grown children of nursing-home residents are always looking for ways to show they care. Your good cheer basket will help them do just that. To make, fill a basket with inexpensive toiletries and candies, and wrap it Easter-basket-style in colorful celluloid. Select imaginative, low-priced items so that, after your mark-up, your basket can be sold for the same price as people are willing to pay for flowers. Show the basket to the nursing-home director, and arrange to display it in the lobby alongside order forms. You may want to donate a certain percentage of each sale to an entertainment fund for the home's residents.

Christmas Magic. If unemployment coincides with the approaching holiday season, you can host a Christmas House. Even though you may not have had time to make crafts yourself, you can invite friends to display their wares in your home for a consignment fee. A warm, fantasy atmosphere, a bowl of hot cider, and fresh gingerbread are all you need to make your home an enticing stop on the craft shopper's trail. Mail invitations to friends and distribute similar announcements throughout the surrounding neighborhoods.

Garage Sale. Properly executed, a garage sale is loaded with moneymaking potential. Advertise in your local newspaper, post attractive signs throughout the neighborhood, and identify your site with colorful flags, streamers, or balloons. Display your goods in eye-pleasing arrangements, write notes describing the suggested use for unusual items, and throw in a few surprises such as fifty-cent grab bags full of goodness-knows-what!

Baked Goods. Some women do very well selling the talents of their kitchen. Homemade breads, pastries, and even catered meals do have a market—just be sure you've located it before you start cooking. Since this money-raising venture requires a health license and a small amount of capital, you should take orders before jumping in. Women's clubs and small restaurants are two good places to start.

OFFER A SERVICE

Baby-sitting. If you like small children, you can offer your services for night and weekend baby-sitting via the local newspaper, church newsletter, and any public bulletin board. You might even try passing the news along to friends by word of mouth. Set a reasonable fee and decide ahead of time whether you'll be willing to go to the customer's home or if it would work best to operate from your own home. Leave the days free, however—baby-sitting is in demand, and if too heavily pursued, could cause you to miss out on important job-related opportunities.

Secretarial Skills/Office Temporaries. Working as a temporary in the secretarial field has always been considered a wise stepping-stone when looking for a more permanent job. Many times, these temporary situations turn into full-time positions. With an ad in your local college or professional school newspaper, you can also work at home typing term papers, etc.

House or Office Cleaning. For those who don't mind burning a little energy by way of elbow grease, housecleaning can be very lucrative. Again, advertising in a local newspaper or by word of mouth will bring you more customers than you can handle.

Odd Jobs. Advertise yourself in the local newspaper as a worker of odd jobs. Busy people will hurriedly latch on to someone who can help around the house or yard.

House-sitter. Watch people's homes while they're away on vacation. Collect mail, water the plants, feed any pets, and make daily checks on the premises. To introduce this service, you may want to design an informal handbill, run it on a copy machine, and deliver to target neighborhoods. Some communities are more liberal about handbill distribution than others. Check with your city government before covering the neighborhood with your name.

Chauffeuring Children. If you own a car in good repair, you can find many busy women willing to pay for the service of taking their children to after-school activities such as dance or music lessons. Again, distributing your homemade handbill in affluent neighborhoods comprised of two-income families is your best bet in locating these women. An announcement on the bulletin board of a large company might also be effective.

EARN MONEY AS A FAMILY

News Delivery Route. Delivering newspapers seems to be a fairly easy job to pick up on short notice. The advantage is that it can usually be completed early in the morning—leaving you free to job hunt the rest of the day.

Can Collecting. Turn a family outing into a small cash-making venture by collecting recyclable aluminum cans. Don't count on big returns—this is not a high-paying job. Your local library will be able to help you locate the nearest recycling center.

Coupon Clipping and Refund Filing. Coupons really do save money! You can organize the whole family into a coupon clipping team. Appoint an older child refund secretary and take advantage of every dollar refund. Setting a weekly time for working on this project will prevent "putting it off" until the dates have expired.

Though it won't help your pocketbook, it may help your morale to think of your job hunt as a temporary career in itself. Use this time to build your support network by contacting friends in the business world, registering at a women's center, and applying at various employment agencies. This is your opportunity to decide what you really want to do with your life. Cherish the privilege.

Most important, appreciate your own individuality. There's a great deal that's right about you. So what if the personnel manager doesn't think you're suited for his job. You *are* right for some job. As a matter of fact, God has a special job just for you that no one else can handle in quite the same way. Sooner or later you're going to meet the right people and the right situation, and all of God's wonderful plans for your life will fall into place. Until then, count your blessings and look on the bright side of life. It's just as easy as looking on the gloomy side, and a whole lot more rewarding!

Be strong and courageous. Do not be terrified; do not be discouraged, for the Lord your God will be with you wherever you go (Joshua 1:9, NIV).

PRACTICAL JOB HUNTING ADVICE

Why fall victim to the job hunt—when you can take control by following a few basic but well-respected steps?

PREPARE A RESUMÉ

Before you even begin looking for a job, you should prepare a resumé. This is your ticket to an interview, and is so important that professional companies get away with charging outlandish fees for preparing them. You don't have to pay someone to write yours. Good resumés follow a concise pattern reproducible by anyone willing to do the work.

There are two basic resumé forms—the work experience resumé and the skill-based resumé. Because each has a specific use, you'll want to define your job-search goal before selecting the resumé style. The work experience resumé is used when you are seeking a different position within the same organization or within your current industry, or when you desire career advancement in the same or similar field. To successfully use this resumé form, you should have a solid work history with no unexplainable employment gaps.

When you are making a career change, reentering the job market, or have a very short career history such as student work during college, the skill-based resumé will help you present yourself in the best light. In this form, you're selling what you do, not who you are. Such a resumé can and should be fun to read and somewhat unique in flavor. Because this is the form to be used by those reentering the job market, it's important to realize that your resumé should not contain apologies for having taken time out to be a mother. As the saying goes, "Every mother is a working mother."

Preparing the Work Experience Resumé

1. Identification: List your name, address, home telephone number, and work telephone number.
2. Job objective: Briefly describe your job-search goal.
3. Background summary: Identify past functions and responsibilities that support your employment objectives.
4. Education: List degrees earned. Dates are not necessary unless they explain gaps in work history.
5. Work history: List employers in chronological sequence, beginning with the most recent. Give the dates of employment, the name and address of employer, your title, and a brief description of your responsibilities. If space permits, it's a nice touch to list a few key accomplishments that are relevant to your job objective. Such accomplishments should begin with action words such as: created, directed, developed, evaluated, etc.
6. Miscellaneous: You may include professional associations to which you belong, publications you've written for, and personal information such as marital status and health status if you like. Height, weight, and age are not necessary.
7. References: Though you don't need to list references on your resumé, be sure you carry their names and addresses with you to your interview.

SAMPLE WORK EXPERIENCE RESUMÉ

1
Jane Doe
401 Brown Street
Arlington, TX 76011
Home: (817) 555-8978
Work: (817) 555-9080

2
JOB OBJECTIVE:	To utilize my writing, editing, and public relations skills in a position that offers challenge and opportunity for advancement based upon performance.

3
BACKGROUND SUMMARY:	I have three years' experience in advertising, including creative writing and concepting, as well as a variety of support services. I have performed on both vendor and client sides of the business and have had office-management responsibility. Thoroughly convinced of the potential of communication in today's world, I have many skills to bring to the marketplace.

4
EDUCATION:	Bachelor of Arts in Communication (Journalism), The University of Texas at Arlington.

Preparing the Skill-Based Resumé

1. Identification: Place your name, address, and telephone numbers at the top of the page.
2. Career objective: Briefly state your job-search goal.
3. Background summary: Review responsibilities and experi-

5

WORK HISTORY:

1982-1984   ABC Carpet Mills
                 3424 East Street, Dallas, TX 76018
                 Sales Promotion Supervisor
                 Responsibilities included participation
                 in creative planning, writing and pro-
                 duction of various elements of sales
                 promotion, merchandising programs
                 and company projects/services.

1981-1982   XYZ—Advertising and Corporate
                     Communications
                 5555 West Street, Dallas, TX 76018
                 Writer and Publications Editor
                 Responsibilities included writing,
                 administration, client contact, and
                 creative concepting for publications,
                 print ads, direct mail, public relations,
                 promotions, brochures, and other
                 collateral materials.

1981   Free-lance writer
                 Contributing Editor, *Fort Worth Woman*.
                 Also published work in the *Dallas
                 Times Herald*, *Campus Imagery*, *Virtue*,
                 Guideposts, and numerous inspira-
                 tional magazines.

6

MISCELLANEOUS: Member of Sigma Delta Chi
               Member of Women in Communications

7

REFERENCES: Available on request
SALARY RANGE: $_ _,000 to $_ _,000

---

ences that support your strengths in relation to your
career goal.
4. Accomplishments: List significant accomplishments that
   illustrate your capabilities for the employment objective.
5. Experience: List dates of employment, name of company,
   and titles held.

6. Education and training: List degrees or special training. If you have none, simply omit.
7. Miscellaneous: List professional organizations to which you belong. You may state personal information such as marital status, if you wish. Omit birth date, height, and weight.
8. References: Mention that references are available, then be sure to carry their names and addresses with you to your interview.

SAMPLE SKILL-BASED RESUMÉ

1

	Sue Brown
66 Summer Street	Home phone: (212)817-6452
New York, NY 10017	Business phone: (212) 543-2929

2

CAREER OBJECTIVE:	Office Manager

3

BACKGROUND SUMMARY:	Nine years' experience in supervising office duties of volunteer health agency.

4

ACCOMPLISHMENTS:	Helped plan and coordinate mailing of 100,000 pamphlets for inner-city health campaign.
	Interviewed and selected volunteers for organization.
	Member on committee to design and implement training of volunteers.

5

EXPERIENCE:	1975-present: City Health Volunteer recruiter and trainer.
	1970-75: Homemaker—mother to three children.

8

REFERENCES:	Available on request

WHEN RESUMÉS DO MORE HARM THAN GOOD

Employers give these reasons for not being favorably impressed with an applicant's resumé.

- Failure of applicant to read the ad. Many people seem to be applying for a position other than the one advertised. It won't work!
- Empty boasts within the resumé. Some people include phrases such as, "my knowledge in this field is vast." A detailed description of one's responsibilities says it much better.
- Gaps in an applicant's work history. Employers say it's better to state that you stayed at home to care for a child, or that you went to school, than to leave a gap.
- Use of current employer's letterhead. Employers view this practice as a mild form of theft.
- Inability to meet elementary standards of good writing. Employers say punctuation, spelling, and grammatical errors point to carelessness.

Resumé trends seem to come and go. What employers like to see now may not be popular in a few years. To be sure that your techniques are the latest, purchase an inexpensive book on the subject—making sure it's a very recent release! Your resumé should be expertly typed and can be further enhanced by being typeset. Have a good number of copies made—a hundred isn't too many. Spelling must be correct—regardless of whether you'll especially need to utilize that skill in your job. More than one woman's unsuccessful job hunt was the result of a misspelled word blaring out from the middle of her resumé!

PREPARING FOR THE INTERVIEW QUESTIONS
Once your resumé has crossed its destined threshold and you're in line for an interview, it's time to think about what's ahead. Spend some time preparing yourself emotionally by visualizing yourself in the following ways:

1. Walking briskly with good posture.
2. Breathing freely and easily.
3. Smiling warmly and making eye contact.
4. Expressing feeling easily.
5. Speaking up.
6. Being the ice-breaker.
7. Thinking positive thoughts.

Imagine questions that are sure to be fired your way. Some favorites are:

1. *Tell me about yourself.*
   Begin with something you're proud of. You may even verbalize this with a statement such as, "Well, there're a lot of things about me that make me well-suited for this job. One of the things I'm most proud of, however, is

   _____

2. *What did you like most about your last job?*
   Mention something you've learned. Be loyal to your present employer up to the last, even if you're unhappy.
3. *What are your strengths and weaknesses?*
   In giving your strengths, "knock 'em dead." Tell them all those wonderful things about yourself—that you're enthusiastic, dependable, skilled, motivated, etc. But when it comes to the weaknesses, disguise a fault as a positive trait. Say something such as, "I'm so motivated that once I get into a project, I tend to let everything else go until I'm finished."
4. *Where do you hope to be in five years?*
   Be honest. Let your ambition show. If you're really uncertain, you can state that you hope to have improved your job skills considerably and to be a more valuable employee.

Another important aspect of the interview is simply convincing the interviewer that you want the job, that you're worth the company's time and money to train. One supervisor almost dismissed an applicant because the applicant didn't come across as wanting the job. "When the woman called back and said she was really interested, I was shocked," the supervisor related. "I had already placed her file back in the cabinet. As it turned out, I ended up hiring the woman and received an excellent employee that I might have otherwise overlooked."

PREPARING YOURSELF
Everyone seriously desiring a professional-level job should invest in a suit. How well I know! I went on my first interviews dressed like a young schoolgirl—pretty summer dress, high heels, and shiny yellow combs in my hair. By the time I was being called back for those second interviews, a good friend had taken me aside and taught me a few tricks . . . mainly, that a professional woman should look and act the part. To accomplish this goal, you need:

■ A conservative suit—preferably multiseasonal
■ Pumps of moderate height—polished to a high gleam
■ Makeup, properly applied—neither over- nor underdone
■ A purse or small briefcase—never both (unless purse fits *inside* briefcase)

It's true that first impressions aren't fair. As Christian women, we need to train ourselves not to judge people solely on first impressions. That doesn't mean, however, that people always will give *you* a second chance. Don't miss out on a God-given opportunity for lack of preparation. Go out there and make the most of what you are.

FROM MY JOURNAL

Heather goes off to an amuse-ment park with $10 in her pocket; comes back with none.

"What did you do with your money?" I ask.

"I bought a Coke," she says.

"A Coke? But what else? I sent you with $10!"

Heather looks pensively into the distance. "Oh," she says, "now I remember. I bought a balloon for $2.50—a great big silver one."

"Where is it?"

"I let it go. It looked so pretty floating up in the air."

I take a deep breath. Where do I begin? How do I teach the concept of austerity to a child whose every whim is provided for by birthright? She is, you see, a child of the "working" rich. A child born to a genera-tion of adults who believe children should have every-thing—just because our parents "almost" gave it all to us.

Suddenly Christ's message on wealth carries new weight for me.

". . . it is easier for a camel to go through the eye of a needle than for a rich man to enter the kingdom of God" (Matthew 19:24, NIV).

". . . but with God all things are possible" (Matthew 19:26, NIV).

And so now I have to strive for the possible.

LIVING SIMPLY:

TWO

Enough Is Never Enough

"We're trying to teach our children an appreciation for hard work and what it can do for you," a physician friend told my husband. "They have no idea what their backyard swimming pool, country club membership, and designer clothes represent in the way of work . . . they've never known it any other way."

Well, at least I can say my child *has* known it otherwise. She's worn second-hand clothes and eaten beans five days a week right alongside her father and me. But even during those difficult medical school years, I always found a way to give Heather "more than enough." And, of course, now there's another problem, which I suspect a great many American families are facing today. How do we retain the values of austerity in the midst of upward mobility?

There is nothing wrong with success; God wants his children to be successful.

"Do not let this Book of the Law depart from your mouth; meditate on it day and night, so that you may be careful to do everything written in it. Then you will be prosperous and successful" (Joshua 1:8, NIV).

But simply to "be" successful is not enough. Our strongest energy and drive should be centered on *living* successfully. And there *is* a difference.

My mother once told me that she figured I'd always lead a successful life. "I don't mean that I think you're going to be rich," she clarified, "but I can tell you're going to be successful."

I knew exactly what she meant. I knew that living successfully didn't mean one always had plenty of money, was continuously in good health, and never suffered emotional aches and pains. I understood the success which she alluded to was the ability to make sound decisions, to move forward instead of looking back, and to go to bed at the end of the day knowing you have done your best. Somehow, even in the early years of our marriage (when we seemed to be the only ones in our circle without money), I knew that there would never be "enough" of the new cars and bigger houses— because only the Bread of Life is truly enough. And later, when I held a high-paying job in the advertising industry but didn't have a minute to spare for my family and God, I began to see again that if we want to move upward in the truest sense, our greatest aspiration must lie in loving the Lord.

I don't know why it is easier to center our thoughts on God when our life takes on elements of simplicity . . . perhaps it's that simplicity seems to slow the tempo of living. But I do know that—in the truest expression of our love for God— people, time, and peace of mind must take precedence over the hurried pace of moneymaking. How you handle this in your own home is basically individual preference. I've chosen to practice simplicity in the midst of plenty as a means of minimizing *thing* worship. I haven't adopted this stance with the belief that we would become more righteous or holy by sacrificing certain luxuries. I just have felt that spending more prudently would make the entire family better stewards of what God has given us . . . and that not spending indiscriminately would help us realize we don't always have to be running after the dollar.

It isn't difficult to fall into the trap of working to live instead of vice versa. But because this statement is just the opposite of what many people propose, let me explain. . . .

I recently heard a woman say the only real reason she worked was to have money to spend on her two days off each week.

It made me wonder if there weren't a number of us who need to reevaluate our motives for working. If it's just for the collecting of things, and our children are still young—we need to be awfully careful. Young children don't care anything about status symbols, and the pursuit of luxuries can burden us with twice the labor. It may be easier, for instance, to carry out the trash each day than to earn the payments for a trash compactor.

Labor not to be rich (Proverbs 23:4, KJV).

Furthermore, if work is not an exciting, exhilarating part of our lives, chances are, God has something better for us in mind. Continuing down the wrong path will only result in overspending on "rewards" for yourself, guilt-gifts for the children, and extravagant convenience goods to make life more bearable.

But there is another reason today's children should not live too pampered a life-style. We don't know the world our children will enter as adults. I look around me and notice that the people who are having the most difficult struggles through adulthood are the ones who were spoiled as children. In fact, many of these adults are still being subtly supported by Mom and Dad's generous gift of a new car or a house payment now and then. Consequently, Mom and Dad are often asking, "Should I still be taking responsibility for my grown child?" My answer would be, "You bet!" When we haven't equipped our children to face whatever world is out there at maturity—we are still very much responsible for their welfare.

HINTS FOR LIVING SIMPLY
IN THE MIDST OF PLENTY

1. Give each child in your family a weekly allowance from which all of his expenditures must come—lunch, treats, toys, etc. It should not be so much that he can com-

fortably purchase ice cream every day and a toy each weekend. Allow your child the sense of worth that comes from sacrificing for a particular purchase; let him do without the ice cream for a few weeks in order to buy that longed-for toy!

2. Reflect simplicity in your own actions. School party favors, birthday cakes, and even gifts can be homemade to make a statement about the art of giving and spending.

3. Stop carrying credit cards, even though you can well afford to charge. Paying with cash forces us to look at our impending purchases in a more realistic light.

4. Give away outgrown clothes. Shop for play clothes at resale clothing shops.

5. Encourage your children to have a toy sale at least once a year. This cleans out their closets while recycling outgrown toys.

6. Teach gratitude. Let your life be a constant expression of gratitude for your material abundance. Never allow yourself or your children to forget your total dependence upon God.

> *. . . our only power and success comes from God*
> (2 Corinthians 3:5b, TLB).

7. Be generous to others—not just to well-known charitable organizations, but to door-to-door salesmen, to girls selling Girl Scout cookies, boys selling school carnival tickets, and so on. Share what you have—your children will pick up on your generous spirit and do likewise.

8. Encourage your school and church to sponsor activities such as family game nights or pot-luck dinners in lieu of field trips to expensive amusement parks or other overpriced entertainment.

9. Discourage fund-raising projects for unnecessary items. For example: Do children's athletic teams really need professional uniforms?

10. Help children and other adults understand the value in doing instead of buying. Rather than purchasing T-shirts for an organization, for instance, let children

bring an old shirt and learn to silkscreen. Instead of
paying costly printing fees for organizational promotions,
show the club how much fun designing and making your
own invitations, announcements, etc., can be.

YOU'VE GOT THE JOB—NOW LOOK THE PART

Very often the pleasure of landing a new job can be
diminished by the thought, "But I haven't anything to wear!"

Susan found herself in just such a predicament. After
several years of attending college and caring for two preschoolers, she had recently been hired as marketing assistant for a
large corporation. Most of her clothes were casual and de-
signed for the role of student/housewife. But now she needed
a smart, authoritative look that would help declare her
serious career intentions—without breaking the family
budget.

Susan didn't want to purchase her wardrobe on credit—
what if the job didn't work out? Nor could she afford a huge
cash outlay—most of it was already earmarked for essentials.
But how could she present a professional image in blue jeans
and big shirt?

After talking to working friends and browsing through
stacks of fashion magazines, Susan discovered that her
situation was not nearly as hopeless as she had thought. All
she really needed to get started on the job were two skirts and
soft shirt combinations, one jacket (as soon as possible she
would add a velvet one which would work for both day
and night), and two shirtwaist dresses. Later, perhaps after
that first paycheck arrived, she would begin the process of
building a true working wardrobe.

Getting a new job or promotion calling for very different
wardrobe standards is enough to make any of us panic. But
it's important to remain sensible and clear-headed about
spending money before it's been earned. Besides, who would
really want to arrive on a new job looking as if a closet of new
clothes had just fallen on her, anyway?

Barbara Coffey, author of *Glamour's Success Book*, suggests
that when you can't afford to purchase a lot of clothes, but do
need versatility, you should invest in separates that can be

paired to look like suits. For instance, a blazer-type jacket could be selected in a color that will go with skirts and dresses you already own. To create the suit look, wear a soft shirt or a turtleneck sweater beneath the jacket.

Working for several weeks before making additional purchases will enable you to buy with wisdom and restraint. But your shopping success can be further enhanced by taking this businesslike approach.

First, identify your needs. Perhaps you're a young professional with a closet full of preppy college clothes. Your immediate needs may be silk blouses to replace the oxford cloth. If your job requires a lot of travel, you may need a couple of neutral wool suits that won't easily wrinkle. Uncertain of your style? Consider consulting a Christian wardrobe consultant who will help match your personality to job clothing requirements for the perfect "look."

Once you have determined your specific needs, write them in a notebook designated for wardrobe planning.

Next, examine your existing wardrobe. Go through your closet with a critical eye. If you don't like a particular garment or haven't worn it in a year, throw it into the rummage sale stack. If you know why you haven't worn it, make a note of this so you won't repeat the mistake. Notice which items need a special accessory or the addition of a blouse or skirt in order to work. Record these needed purchases in your notebook.

Now experiment with what you have. Spend an afternoon or morning trying on clothes you already own. Mix and match color combinations, add scarves, jewelry, belts, and shoes. Look through current magazines for new ways to wear the old. Write or sketch these combinations and ideas in your notebook.

At last you're ready to shop.

SHOPPING HINTS

1. Avoid impulse shopping. If it's not exactly what you're looking for, pass it up—no matter what the price.
2. If you need something to go with a particular garment

you own, put it in a bag and take it shopping with you to ensure a perfect match.

3. To get the most for your money, make sure the color of your new purchase works with other garments or accessories, including shoes and jewelry.

4. Try mass volume or discount stores, but look discriminately. It's often possible to find a really superior garment among rows and rows of poorer quality merchandise.

5. Remember the importance of proper fit. Too tight a fit will ruin your professional look.

6. Purchase a book on dressing for work and use it as a guideline for selecting colors and styles that will enhance your particular work image.

7. Purchase good quality clothes in classic styles. You'll be able to wear them for several years, knowing that they still look good. Keep them in one or two basic colors and you won't tire of them. You can always add excitement with a brightly colored blouse, scarf, or accessories.

8. Learn to sew if you don't already know how. Unless you're an accomplished seamstress, stay with simple lines and copy the fabric and color illustrated on the pattern jacket.

9. Hunt for interesting accessories at garage sales. Scarves to drape around your hips or shoulders, handkerchiefs to stuff into your suit pocket, and tasteful jewelry are all possible finds that will inexpensively complement your wardrobe.

10. Purchase pretty, color-coordinated purse accessories to help keep the contents of your handbag tidy and organized.

STRETCH YOUR WARDROBE

By sticking to one or two color schemes in your clothes, you can coordinate accessories and easily mix and match your outfits. In the book *Working Wardrobe*, Janet Wallach shows how to use twelve pieces of clothing in two colors (black/red) for the stunning total of forty-eight different looks!

WHAT *NOT* TO WEAR TO THE OFFICE

- See-through clothing. Camisoles or full slips should be worn beneath sheer blouses.
- Tight, obviously sexy clothes.
- Pants—unless your job requires them for the type of work you do.
- Sundresses or resort-type clothing.
- Fancy, evening-type fabrics.

CLOTHES CARE

AT WORK:

- Perk up shoes with a drop of hand cream and buff with an old powder puff.
- Cover scuff marks on white shoes with white typewriter correcting fluid.
- Keep a survival kit in your desk drawer. In a small cosmetic bag keep a small container of makeup, a needle, basic colors of thread, and safety pins.

AT HOME:

- Remove work clothes upon your arrival home. Hang up immediately. Air for several hours before placing in your closet.
- Hang heavy clothes on heavy hangers. If you can't afford wooden hangers just yet, take two or three wire hangers and tape them across the bottom and at the neck.
- At the end of each season, examine clothes and shoes for needed repairs. Attend to repairs, then put away in clean condition.
- Plan work outfits a week in advance. Choose accessories and press your selected garments.

IF YOU'RE A FREQUENT TRAVELER

Business trips are commonly required of working women these days. But while many of us have been packing our husband's "carry-on" bag for years, we're still struggling with the concept of packing lightly for ourselves. In fact, a business trip is likely to find us standing in the baggage claim area, wilting under a load of heavy luggage. The unprofessional look itself should be enough to frighten us into learning the art of traveling light. But there are some even more important reasons for living out of one "carry-on" bag during business trips.

1. You will have no fear of losing your luggage en route.
2. If timing from the airport to the meeting is vital, you waste no time at the baggage claim area.
3. When traveling with men, who will most likely carry only one bag, you'll fit into the group's plans more easily if not hampered by an armload of luggage. Besides, unless the men are very courteous, they will generally catch a cab and leave you at the baggage claim area alone—making it appear that you arrived at the meeting late.

My sister Barbra's job takes her on frequent business trips—usually of two to three days' duration. To get by on a minimum of clothing and fuss, she recommends following these guidelines.

1. Study your itinerary. Check a large newspaper such as the *New York Times* for weather reports of your destination and think in terms of those whom you have come to meet. Meeting with the same people over several days will require more clothing changes than meeting with a variety of different people.
2. Make a clothing plan. Barbra takes one basic-colored suit for a three-day trip. She coordinates it with a blouse, a sweater, a dress shirt, and a silk tie. For greater versatility, she packs an extra pair of shoes—wearing the lower-heeled pair while traveling and the dressier pair for appointments the next day.
3. Make a list. Barbra's looks something like this:

1 blouse	1 robe and gown
1 sweater	1 pair slippers
1 pair extra nylons	1 jogging suit (for wearing
1 pair dress shoes	in hotel room)
1 travel iron	1 cosmetic kit
1 stain remover	

All of this is packed in a hanging bag, which can be carried onto the plane with you. Hang what you would ordinarily hang; place folded items and cosmetics in the bottom.

Happy landing!

SPECIAL NOTE!

If the amount of time put into organizing your wardrobe seems inconsistent with Christian principles, reconsider your ultimate goal. An orderly, attractive wardrobe frees your mind and time for more important things such as early morning Bible study, and enables you to represent the Christian community with dignity.

QUESTIONS WORKING MOTHERS ASK
THE OFFICE EAT-IN

QUESTION
Someone at work is always having a baby or celebrating some other type of milestone that calls for baked goods or a lunch-time casserole. What do I do—run myself ragged after work filling orders, or ignore the pleas for help and look un-friendly?

ANSWER
You don't have to do either. Your choices are (1) Stop by the bakery and purchase the goods; or, (2) Select simple recipes that call for very little cooking and cleanup. If you opt for the first choice, you can easily replace the bakery's white box with your own plate and plastic wrap. Though you have nothing to hide, your own plate will attract less attention in such circumstances and probably make you feel more com-fortable. Another approach is simply to serve the food in its bakery container with no apologies or remorse about not having time to cook. After all, you're a working woman. Your first priority when on the job is getting the work done—not entertaining other office employees. As for casseroles, you can solve this problem easily enough by becoming known as the dessert lady. Tell the party's organizer that you're happy to help with dessert, but simply can't manage a main dish. In

no time at all, people will be enthusiastically asking you to make your "house" specialty.

QUICK AND EASY BAKED GOODS

MACAROONS

5⅓ cups (14-oz. bag) flake coconut
1 can sweetened condensed milk
2 teaspoons vanilla
Combine all ingredients. Drop from teaspoon about one inch apart on a well-greased baking sheet. Decorate with sprinkles or maraschino cherries. Bake at 350° for 10-12 minutes or until lightly browned. Immediately remove from baking sheet using moistened spatula. Makes about 5 dozen.

FUDGIES

2 cups sugar
2 tablespoons cocoa
½ cup evaporated milk
½ cup margarine
1½ teaspoons vanilla
3 cups uncooked oatmeal
Mix sugar, cocoa, and milk in saucepan. Add margarine and heat on stove, bringing to boil. Add vanilla and oatmeal. Stir until oats look like chocolate candy, and pour into buttered pan. Serving numbers vary, depending upon size of cookies—but this recipe provides a generous plateful, regardless.

HELLO DOLLIES

½ cup margarine
1 cup chocolate chips
1 cup flake coconut
1 cup vanilla wafer crumbs
1 cup chopped pecans
1 cup sweetened condensed milk
Preheat oven to 350°. Melt margarine in 8" x 8" pan. Add remaining ingredients in layers in order as listed. Bake 25-30 minutes or until golden brown. Makes about two dozen bar cookies.

PARENTAL SCHOOL INVOLVEMENT

QUESTION

My son's school is forever asking parents to work in carnival booths, collect newspapers, bake cakes, or cook hamburgers for various fund-raising drives. I don't want to appear uninterested—for both my son's and the school's sake; but since I don't have time for these activities, I find myself resenting them. Is there a good way to say no?

ANSWER

Schools often make a working mother feel less than adequate with their numerous requests for parental involvement. Working mothers can't sew costumes, take part in telephone chains, and bake cakes like their nonworking sisters. But there are other options. The next time you feel pressed to offer your help, consider the many business-related services you might be able to offer. Free printing, a supply of envelopes, samples, or even a financial lead should make a lot more sense than struggling with the contribution of a cake. Just don't give away anything that's not within your jurisdiction to do so!

QUESTION

Our child's teacher invariably schedules conferences during peak work hours. Not only is it embarrassing to ask off, it's highly frowned upon in my company. How can I get the teacher to be more sensitive toward my situation?

ANSWER

School conferences are a dilemma for both teachers and mothers. Keep in mind that the teacher doesn't want to work after hours either! The easiest solution is for both parents to alternate taking off for these conferences. But another approach is to face the issue head-on. Write a note to your child's teacher explaining that while you are interested in your child's progress, a conference scheduled during work hours means loss of income for you, or loss of respect from your boss—neither one satisfactory. Ask if the conference couldn't be scheduled before 8:00 A.M. or as close to 5:00 P.M. as possible. As a last resort, consider arranging a telephone conference after work. Do carry on such a conversation in your bedroom with the door shut, so that you will have the same privacy you would encounter in a school conference.

MAINTAINING FRIENDSHIPS

QUESTION
My friends are some of my most valuable resources, yet now that I'm working, I find them slipping away one by one. How can I find time for these people who mean so much to me?

ANSWER
It's wise to recognize the importance of friendship in a working woman's life. Friends not only support and add balance to our lives, they are very often God's instruments in helping us grow. At first glance it may seem you have merely traded friends from one area of your life for the people you work with. But look carefully. Work relationships can be superficial, and acquaintances are not necessarily friends. Besides a husband to talk to, we still need a good woman friend whom we can confide in and trust. But to keep in touch with such a person requires a sincere desire and effort on both people's part. And because one person will have to make the first move—it might as well be you.

Begin by making a list of all the friends you need to make contact with. Try making one date a week, going down the list until you've visited with each one. Some things you can do:

- When a friend works nearby, a quick lunch at a fast-food restaurant may be all you need to reconnect. But if you're not allowed an occasional extended lunch hour, the complications of such a meeting can be enormous and perhaps not worth the risk to your job.
- If your friend has children, you may opt for dinner at a family pizza restaurant which offers the children grand entertainment, while giving adults an opportunity to talk. (Make sure your husband's taken care of before leaving, however.)
- Ask a friend to join you in the purchase of season tickets to a sports event or the theater. If your budget allows, a gift of such a ticket would be an especially thoughtful gesture.
- Keep a birthday book in which you list your friends'

■ birthdays and other significant dates. Telephone or mail cards of best wishes on these days. One year a friend surprised me with a birthday gift of a small candle— handsomely wrapped and beribboned. It had been a long time since anyone outside of the family had remembered my birthday, and I was immensely pleased. The incident reminded me how meaningful unexpected friendship gifts can be. Such gifts are usually inexpensive items that are funny, or reminders of good times you've shared as friends.

■ When husbands are also acquainted and compatible, you can invite your friend's entire family to dinner. Hire a baby-sitter to look after both sets of children while the adults prepare dinner together as they enjoy fellowship.

Keep your efforts at maintaining friendships confined to your off-work hours. Remember, it is never appropriate for a friend to merely drop by your place of business. Since some of your friends are certain to be nonworking women and unfamiliar with this rule, arrange ahead of time for the receptionist to hold unexpected visitors in the reception area until you can come forward and explain the situation.

QUIET TIME

QUESTION

I love God's Word and want to study it regularly along with having an in-depth prayer life, but there's never any time. How can I feed my spiritual hunger while juggling family, job, and church?

ANSWER

Good for you—this is what it's all about . . . what makes everything else fall in place. And recognizing the need for spiritual food puts you in an ideal starting position, because for the working mother to find time alone with God requires a genuine dedicated commitment. It won't happen by itself. We have to put aside a definite time and place in our lives for meeting the Lord on a one-to-one basis.

There are probably hidden moments in your current schedule that could become your personal time with God. You'll also discover that a more streamlined, organized life (see Organization: Setting Things Straight) will allow you greater flexibility for a morning or evening quiet time.

Prayer and Bible study require some uninterrupted time— at least fifteen minutes; but I also find it helpful to pause at my desk for a few minutes of silent prayer before beginning work each morning. A more in-depth talk with God can take place during the lunch hour or perhaps during an evening jog. Another secret: I like to keep Scripture cards and prayer lists in my purse. Sometimes the Scripture cards are purchased, sometimes handwritten from my private devotions; but they are always passages which speak to me and uplift me in a special way.

If concentrating on your talk with the Lord is difficult because of a fragmented or cluttered mind, try writing your prayers. Writing is thought provoking and will help you pray more specifically. It is also a valuable tool for looking back and discovering where we've come from to date. A variation of the written prayer is the keeping of a concise prayer journal in which you list your prayer request, the date, and God's answer and the date. This, too, is a means of targeting our thoughts on specifics, and can be exciting proof of God's interaction in our lives when we look back and see how much he has done for us over a period of time.

Sometimes we want these special moments with God; but in the midst of go, go, go—we completely forget about taking that prearranged or hidden time to be alone with our Savior. To help us remember our goal, we can go on an occasional lunch fast. Drink fruit juices and read the Bible during this hour. (Plan on a slow afternoon and perhaps a carryout dinner from a fast-food restaurant for the family that night.)

Finally, follow a meaningful Bible study program that you can relate to. It's easy to become discouraged with Bible reading if it doesn't seem to correspond with today's problems and challenges. I enjoy Joyce Marie Smith's Bible studies (Tyndale House) which explore woman-centered topics and concerns.

FROM MY JOURNAL

When Heather plays dolls, I notice a strange thing. She carefully dresses them in freshly washed clothes, combs their shiny acrylic hair, gives them a loving pat on the head, and takes them to a pretend day-care center in the corner of her room. Heather then turns off her bedroom lamp, closes the door to her room, and heads for the outdoors where she rides bikes or jumps rope.

The first time I witnessed this phenomenon, I was shocked. I have worked in some capacity since Heather's birth, but the fact that I had presented my child with such a strong image of part-time mothering was greatly distressing.

Today I think differently. From the carefree smiles Heather displays during her play, I can only assume that a working mother has very positive connotations with my daughter. She is, after all, of another generation. Heather already knows that while mommies often work, it's still their responsibility to see that their children have fresh clothing and shiny clean hair, and receive plenty of soothing physical strokes whenever possible.

Heather's grown-up life will have fewer harsh surprises in this regard than mine did.

CHILD CARE:

THREE

God Bless the Children

I met up with Karen at the central copy machine one day at work. Heavy with child, she was due for maternity leave at the end of the week.

"What about child care?" I asked inquisitively. "Have you got it all set up?"

Karen looked startled.

"No," she said. "There are so many little kids in our neighborhood, and everybody works—so, I just don't see baby-sitting as a big deal. I mean, all of those kids have to be taken care of by someone!"

Some time later, Karen had the baby and returned to work after the appropriate six-week interval. And, sure enough, life had turned out to be blissfully easy—the woman next door was caring for little John. I was almost jealous, remembering all the sitters and child-care centers I'd gone through in the past years . . . and none of them next door!

But a few weeks later, Karen joined the rest of us in the real world. It seemed her neighbor no longer wanted to keep an infant.

"Now what do I do?" I overheard her tearfully asking another woman.

"You worry a lot," the woman answered drily.

Karen smiled through her tears. But I didn't. For in truth, the woman had spoken volumes. Child-care arrangements are probably the working mother's number one concern. So important is the relationship between a satisfactory child-care arrangement and a woman's job performance, that finding child care should be approached as seriously as the job hunt itself.

Where does one look for competent, affordable child care? A lot will depend upon geographic location and income. For instance, those New York City nannies sound terribly good to those of us in the Midwest, but not at all realistic. They'd require more than half of our salary! Nor does suburban life help matters. What with its lack of public transportation, we even have a difficult time enticing the younger and older women from our area to come out each day. So, we usually do a lot of "asking around," following hunches, and reading between the lines. Sound familiar? If so, here are a few important considerations to help you base your child-care decision on sound, reasonable expectations.

Know your alternatives. The choice is not strictly between expensive nannies and budget child-care centers. Investigate every option in your area—carefully weighing the pros and cons of each.

ALTERNATIVES:
Mother's helper—a good answer for the part-time employee.

These women usually don't want to work full time, but will often do light housework as well as look after your child. To find such a person, advertise in a college newspaper or the local shopper. You'll probably discover she's willing to accept minimum wage or less.

Relatives—Grandparents make especially wonderful care-takers, *if* they're available. Besides, their services are usually free, and grandparents can give your child a keen sense of security. To avoid friction, you must be willing to relinquish your child during these hours—advice easier given than done, particularly if you're depending upon in-laws who may do things very differently from you.

Baby-sitter—Baby-sitters are most often found through local newspapers or by word of mouth. Those who require you to bring your child to their house will usually be priced a little

under the going day-care center rate. If you must have someone in your home, be prepared to pay a great deal more.
However, you can be creative in how you meet this expense.
One woman I know shares her baby-sitter with the woman
next door. One week the baby-sitter comes to my friend's
house and the neighbor brings her child over. The next week,
the arrangement is reversed.

Probably the most crucial problem in dealing with private
baby-sitters is lack of dependability. To encourage regular
service whether in your home or hers—pay your sitter a tad
more than average and offer a bonus for "no days missed."

Role reversal—Daddy takes on the traditional responsibilities
of Mom under this plan. It seems to work well when the
husband's occupation can be home-based, or when the wife
has the higher income potential. For a child to get to know
his father in such an intimate way is a rare and wonderful
privilege.

Work co-op—Part-time working moms can form a baby-
sitting co-op arranged around their various working
schedules. This requires a fairly large network of friends,
though participants could probably be found through advertising in a local newspaper.

Commercial or church day-care centers—Both should be
judged by the same criteria. And neither need be feared
strictly on the basis of adverse publicity. Common sense and
a watchful eye can help keep your child safe in a day-care
setting.

Choosing the right center in the first place is a big advantage. Although you shouldn't hesitate for a moment about
withdrawing your child from a suspicious environment,
remember that frequent day-care hopping is hard on the
child. If finding the right place is taking longer than you
expected, contact your future employer and request another
week before coming to work. You don't have to say why—
something about taking care of business matters will suffice.

To help you make your decision, here are some simple
guidelines to follow.

Check for:
1. Clean, spacious playrooms.
2. Fenced playgrounds with climbing equipment.
3. Nutritious lunches.
4. A cot and blanket for each child.
5. A teacher for every eighteen children.
6. A safe environment—with no ungated stairways, open doors to the street, or accessible cleaning agents.
7. A willingness by the staff to show you around at any time. While it's true the director may need to make an appointment with you to discuss fees, your request to look around the premises should be pleasantly honored. Closed doors or "forbidden" areas are red flags. (The least you can expect to find behind them is hidden filth.)

Ideally, a day-care teacher should be affectionate, articulate, patient, creative, and enthusiastic. But what it really boils down to is that few day-care centers pay enough to attract such people. You'll have to be willing to compensate by providing lots of extra attention at home. One way to know whether you've made the right decision is by observing how eager your child is to leave each morning.

TO MAKE THINGS EASIER . . .

You *can* help your child adjust to the new day-care situation. Here are some pointers.

1. Try out the arrangement before you begin work. Start part time and build up to full days.
2. Provide your child with a link to home, such as a blanket or a favorite toy.
3. Arrive fifteen minutes early in the morning. This prevents the feeling of being hurriedly dumped, and helps your child get reoriented to his daytime environment.
4. Help your child make a special friend by inviting another child from the center to play at your house on the weekend.
5. Watch for signs of extreme distress: excessive crying or clinging, reverting to immature behavior, bed wetting, thumb sucking, head banging, etc.

THINGS TO ALWAYS KEEP IN MIND

1. Never threaten to leave your child at the center as punishment.
2. Always be on time for evening pickup. Try to come early every once in a while.
3. To ensure that all is well, make periodic unexpected visits.
4. Remember that day-care needs change as a child grows. Young children need physical care—older children need a sense of companionship. Parents of older children recommend making certain that teenagers become involved in after-school activities such as volunteer work, baby-sitting, music or drama lessons, and so forth. Summer calls for camp and extensive visiting of relatives.

Even with the child-care issue solved, you'll still have moments of doubt—when you question the decision to work in the first place. It may help to talk to the mothers of older children. They'll tell you that children who spend the day away from Mom don't turn out so badly after all. While they don't have the exclusive nurturing of Mother, they do learn to turn to other adults and to be sensitive to the needs of other children. They develop especially self-sufficient and outgoing personalities. And they grow up knowing that a woman can and should contribute to society just as she does at home. The final word from experts is that children of working mothers are pretty much like the children of nonworking mothers.

Jay Belsky, director of the Pennsylvania Infant and Family Development Project, summed it up for an article in *McCall's* magazine (January 1985) when he said, "Children the world over grow up in a variety of circumstances and do just fine."

Christian mothers can also take heart in the fact that our children are cared for and watched over even in our absence.

"For I tell you that their angels in heaven always see the face of my Father in heaven" (Matthew 18:11, NIV).

FROM MY JOURNAL

It's Tuesday. Heather and I arrive at school feeling very proud of ourselves—we've remembered everything . . . Brownie dues, lunch, homework, and an empty box for an art project.

Heather bounces out of the car, eager to start the day because, for once, she is on top of things.

"Did you remember your box?" she asks, running up to Cindy.

Cindy is a delightful, bubbly blonde who reacts to crisis in my own true style.

"Oh, no, oh, no," she wails, dropping to her knees and hitting her head with her hands.

"Did you remember your box?" Heather now asks of Cara.

"Oh, oh, oh," tiny Cara grabs her stomach and whines like a wounded animal.

Finally, we see Amber climb out of her family's car. She is walking slowly toward the playground, and though I notice a box tucked under her arm, there is the unmistakable look of gloom upon her face.

"What's wrong?" Heather asks. "You remembered your box. Is it your lunch? Your homework? Your Brownie dues?"

"Oh, no, Heather," the child answers. "This is much worse. The most terrible thing has happened. . . . I've outgrown my Holy Communion dress and communion is next month. My mother squeezed and tugged, but we couldn't get it to fit me."

I stand in the tension-ridden schoolyard feeling sorry and very sad for a generation of children nurtured on the world's distress. How I would like to stop and reach out to these youngsters—to reassure them that it's going to be all right. But I look at my watch and hurry on. With my back to the playground, I am no longer Mommy—I am promotion supervisor. And already, my mind is racing ahead to the day I must face.

Will my boss like the ad campaign I developed yesterday? Why didn't the president of the company drop by to make a pleasant comment about the newsletter like he normally does?

Then, as I pull into the office parking lot, I find myself hoping that the wrong people won't see me slipping in five minutes late. Suddenly I stop. It's early morning and I already have a headache. But that's not the real problem—I am visualizing those children on the playground and recognizing their stress as an inheritance from modern times.

HANDLING STRESS

FOUR

When Times Are Really Bad

Other women saw Marge as the epitome of the successful
working woman. An accountant at a large oil firm, she was
also the mother of two happy children and the wife of a
doting husband. Her work history read like a fairy tale. From
the first day she arrived on the job, Marge had been labeled a
rising star and was carefully groomed by upper management
to one day step in as the company's first woman manager. It
was no secret that Marge was a woman going places, and go
places she did! Within five years, she had earned her CPA
and been promoted to the coveted managerial position for
which she'd been destined. Then suddenly without warning—
just days before stepping into her new role—Marge surprised
everyone by resigning from the company to become a full-
time homemaker. What happened?

"It was the stress," Marge explained. "I just couldn't live
with it—the daily struggle of being all things to all people—
of juggling motherhood with career. I wanted to do so well.
Not just at work, but at home, too. Trouble is, we women have
to learn everything by trial and error, and it didn't take me
long to discover that there was no one to tell me how to do it
all. I woke up each morning afraid I'd fall on my face and
disappoint someone who believed in me at work or someone
who believed in me at home. Then one day I caught myself
thinking in terms of what if I didn't have the children. It was

then I realized that, for me, resigning was the only solution."

Though Marge's reaction to work life may seem a bit drastic, her plight is easily recognizable to any working mother. There's probably not a one of us who hasn't at least thought of chucking it all for a less stressful existence. The feeling that life is about to cave in is normal among working women. But since resigning our jobs isn't always a realistic option, most of us square our shoulders and stoically give in to the symptoms of stress. Depression, headaches, tight muscles in the back or neck, upset stomach, frequent crying, irritableness, diarrhea, constipation, and excessive fatigue all become a part of the working mother's employment package. What's more, studies indicate the higher up the corporate ladder a working mom climbs, the more likely she is to encounter the level of stress which causes these ugly problems.

In a recent article in the *Academy of Management Review*, authors Debra Nelson and James Quick quote studies suggesting professional women experience more stress than housewives or their male counterparts at work. Nelson and Quick state this is probably because professional women not only share common demands with male executives, but suffer additional demands with which men usually don't have to cope—obstacles such as discrimination, stereotyping, conflicting demands of work and marriage, and social isolation.

Born of emotional frustration, these factors are more likely to cause the diseases of stress than are the physical demands which the blue collar employee may experience. But this doesn't mean that only professional working mothers experience stress, nor does it mean that any working mother has to succumb to the diseases of stress. With proper management and understanding, all of us can overcome the problems of stress and enjoy a healthy, productive work and home life.

Let's take a quick look into the background of stress. Stress comes from two basic forces—the physical stress of exercise or hard work and the mental stress of emotional frustration.

The body reacts to stress in three stages: 1) alarm; 2) resistance; and 3) exhaustion. In the alarm stage, our body prepares for "flight or fight." A release of hormones from the endocrine glands will actually cause an increase in heart rate and respiration, elevated blood sugar, increased perspiration, dilated pupils, and slowed digestion. In the resistance stage the body recovers from its initial alarm and repairs any damage caused by it. This takes us to the exhaustion stage, which if continued under stress for a prolonged time, can cause us to develop one of the diseases of stress such as migraine headaches, high blood pressure, or even mental illness.

Doctors tell us there is no way to completely eliminate stress from our lives—nor would we even want to, because a little stress is actually good for us. It's the juice that revs us up for big projects . . . it's the challenge that keeps life from becoming boring. So the object is to learn how to live with stress so that it doesn't become the *dis*-stress which brings about disease.

Working mothers need to recognize several factors. First, it is very difficult to function as a working mother. It doesn't matter how effortlessly the community's supermom appears to glide through life; rest assured, she does so under stress. We have to accept the fact that what we're doing isn't easy and then admit that we may not do it perfectly. There are simply too many uncontrollable variables out there that keep us from coping flawlessly. Nothing *we* do, for instance, will keep the children from waking up with a stomach virus; nor can *we* prevent the boss from reacting out of his own inner turmoil. Our goal should be to cope the best way we can and to direct our energy toward those things that we can control.

One of the best places to start when dealing with the issue of personal stress is your family physician—he handles it daily, both in his own life and his patients'. If you think you may be suffering from stress, have a checkup and ask your doctor for personal guidelines to help you overcome the problem.

With special regard for the Christian working mother's desire to function positively, family physician Dr. Olie Garrison compiled these suggestions for harnessing our stress into productive results. You may want to implement these ideas, or with the help of a health professional come up with your own.

1. *Talk it out.* First with God, then with another human. It really helps to share a problem verbally. Sometimes talking

enables us to see the situation in a more logical sense and we are then able to move on it. At other times, talking merely serves as a release. But try to find a receptive listener whom you can trust and respect. (Preferably not someone from the office.) Though our first thought may be our spouse, he may not be the best choice. Sometimes we are better off with an advocate such as a friend, minister, teacher, doctor, or counselor. There are also certain times of the day which may be better suited for talking about problems than other times. Try to find a time when both you and your advocate are not rushed.

2. *Take care of yourself physically.* Most of us claim to do so, but don't be too sure. The typical working mother rises by 5:00 A.M. It doesn't matter if the baby or a sick child kept her up all night—for her there'll be no afternoon nap. She skips breakfast from being too rushed and eats a greasy taco or hamburger for lunch. Work is difficult. She deals with numbers and there's no room for errors. When her boss criticizes yesterday's performance, she wants to give him a "piece of her mind," but holds back because she needs the job. After work, she has to pick up the children from the child-care facility and stop at the grocery for dinner items. Once home, she prepares and serves dinner, supervises the children's baths, puts them to bed, picks up the house, rereads a report she wrote at work, lays out the family's clothing for the next day, takes her own bath, and falls asleep. She didn't eat much dinner—she was too tired. But she did grab several handfuls of chips throughout the evening. She didn't exercise—there wasn't time. And certainly she didn't mention her frustration about "doing it all" to her husband—that would only start an argument. Besides, it was just an average day in this working mother's life.

3. *Set daily priorities.* Give each daily task a position on your schedule. List what you have to do. Write an A beside the most urgent items, a B beside the less urgent, and a C beside those things that can wait indefinitely. Sometimes it helps to get the most dreaded chore out of the way first. Once it's completed, you'll experience a feeling of relief—or lack of tension.

4. Pay attention to the things that make you feel good. Feel free to enjoy a compliment, being lucky, having good weather, and so on.

5. After a very tense situation, analyze how you coped. There may be a better technique to handle the problem; but if you feel you did well, remember how you reacted so you can use the same technique in similar situations.

6. Delegate what you can. If life is too crowded and there's no end in sight, let other people do some of your work—and not just in the office. Pay someone to make the children's costumes for the school play; hire a teenager to tend to your lawn; order by mail. If you put your mind to it, there are all kinds of ways to unclutter your life.

7. Don't add changes on top of changes. If you've had a major change in your life, don't add more. For instance, if you're moving to a new house in the same town, try to keep your regular job and remain in the same church for awhile.

8. Keep an anti-stress box on hand in the kitchen and in your clothes closet. The kitchen box should contain the necessary ingredients for a complete meal. You don't have to wait for an all-out emergency to use the box—pull it out at the first hint of being in a bind for dinner. The closet box should contain shoes, handbag, stockings, jewelry, and underclothes that you could wear with a suitable garment to just about any function. The next time you have to be there "on the double," you'll arrive on time and serene.

9. Learn to relax. Practice exercises learned in childbirth classes or use this simple technique.
   a. Find a comfortable chair in some quiet part of the house.
   b. Begin to slowly and rhythmically inhale and exhale. Take deep cleansing breaths with each inhalation, being sure to completely expel this breath upon exhalation.
   c. Empty your mind of trivia by concentrating on a particularly pleasant scene or sensation such as

lying on the beach with small waves gently lapping over your body or sitting in a tub of warm water.

d. Imagine your body filled with sand. Now, starting with the forehead and proceeding to your toes, tense and relax the muscles. As you relax each body segment, imagine that portion of your body being emptied of sand.

10. Designate a time and place in your home in which you can be alone. This is your private space and time for relaxation and meditation—use it daily.

11. Smile and make an effort to bring sunshine into the lives of five people you come in contact with throughout the day. Being happy and cheerful will help keep you from feeling stress.

12. Live one day at a time. And if that seems too hard, try getting through one hour at a time. Don't forget, however, as Christians, we have a built-in defense mechanism against dis-stress. This special defense is faith. Faith fills us with peace, and peace is the very ingredient required for a less stressful life.

Therefore, since we have been justified through faith, we have peace with God through our Lord Jesus Christ, through whom we have gained access by faith into this grace in which we now stand (Romans 5:1, NIV).

Faith develops this peace in a number of ways—one of which is enabling us to think positively.

Finally, brothers, whatever is true, whatever is noble, whatever is right, whatever is pure, whatever is lovely, whatever is admirable—if anything is excellent or praiseworthy—think about such things (Philippians 4:8, NIV).

Faith also allows us to slow down—another true pathway to peace. When we believe in eternal life, there's no need to hurry. There's plenty of time for loving those around us and living unselfishly and slowly, because life goes on forever.

Jesus demonstrated such peace by taking time to listen to the woman at the well, taking children into his arms, and telling people that he loved them.

13. Read the Bible for actual instructions on coping with stress. The study of Elijah provides some very useful examples for dealing with this problem.

READ 1 KINGS 19

In this chapter Elijah is in the wilderness facing what seemed to him the end of the world. He was fleeing from Jezebel and had stopped under a tree to await death. He was physically tired and fell into an exhausted sleep. All at once, an angel came to him offering water and bread. Elijah ate, drank, and lay down to rest again.

Step One: When you feel stress coming on, eat something nourishing (even if you're not hungry), drink a big glass of water, and lie down to rest if you can. Stress is physically tiring. Attention to your physical needs will help your body channel energy to the mind.

When Elijah had rested, he traveled to the mountain of Horeb and lived in a cave for awhile.

Step Two: Do something different. Anything. Think back to things that normally make you feel good, select one of these activities, and do one every day. Elijah traveled. Maybe you could take some time off work and visit a relative. Some other ideas:

1. Read in your spare time. Go to the library on Saturday and browse without deadline; visit a bookstore on your lunch break and treat yourself to a purchase.
2. Go window shopping during lunch. Buy something you can afford.
3. Go out to eat.
4. Talk to a friend.
5. Join an exercise class.

Next, Elijah had a real heart-to-heart talk with the Lord. God asked him what he was doing in the mountain cave, and

ON THE JOB

Aside from leaving a too stressful job environment, is there anything that can be done to improve one's work situation? Possibly—if one is really willing to put the necessary effort into the project. Here are a few suggestions for handling some of the unique causes of stress experienced by working mothers.

1. Find a mentor. Quick and Nelson mention mentoring as one of the key moderators of the stress-health relationship. The authors state that when successful businesswomen talk about the forces that helped them achieve—they invariably tell of having mentors. A mentor is a person who takes a special interest in your career. He or she is important because of his established place in the business world and because he can advise you on how to climb the corporate ladder. Second, the mentor displays confidence in you as a female employee, which in turn builds your self-confidence. Third, the mentor knows about stress and can help you deal with it. Obviously, a female mentor would be ideal. But there aren't enough of them around just yet, so you may have to seek guidance from a male executive.

2. Build your self-confidence. Another moderating factor of stress is self-confidence. Quick and Nelson point out that successful career women have self-confident, positive attitudes about themselves and their work environments. They say these women seem to create their own opportunities—that even stress is viewed as an opportunity rather than a threat.

3. Develop self-awareness. Get to know your body and its limits. Experienced runners frequently monitor their physical well-being and adjust their pace to avoid pain or injury. Women can do the same thing with their work life. Perhaps life in the fast lane really is too much. In that case, discover what you can handle at this time in

3. your life. In "Women on the Job," *McCall's,* July 1985, Susan Jacoby tells how a former account executive quit her job after the birth of her first child. The decision was not a mistake. By the time her second child arrived, the woman was working for a small marketing company and was much happier. She had learned to weigh her needs against her physical capabilities. She knew, for instance, that she wanted to work outside the home. But she also realized that for now, the job should not demand more than her family.

   Sometimes self-awareness is a simple matter of saying no, of taking responsibility for you. If you know, for instance, that your energy is waning, you should probably not agree to bake cookies for your child's class party.

4. Learn to laugh about it. In an article by Michael Sleeter in *Working Woman* magazine (October 1981), laughter is cited as an often overlooked pressure-release valve. "Laughter," the author says, "allows an escape of nervous energy; it has a flushing effect on the air in the lungs and on blood circulation."

   You'll also find laughter not only relieves tension, but can be used to drive home a point, illustrate a problem, and build rapport with fellow workers.

5. Accept nurturing from unexpected sources. The company's housekeeper was one of my most valuable friends on one job. Her genuine concern about whether or not my coffee mug was clean and my desk dusted to satisfaction gave me a warm, cared-for feeling that took the rough edges off of "real" problems.

6. Develop assertiveness. Psychologist Arthur Nezu of Farleigh Dickinson University at Teaneck, N.J., surveyed 168 men and women, evaluating, among other things, personal coping strategies. He found people who took an assertive approach to solving their problems were less depressed during stressful experiences.

THE BODY'S RESPONSE TO STRESS

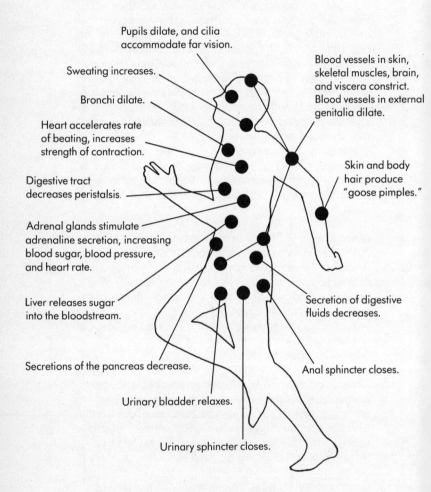

Pupils dilate, and cilia accommodate far vision.

Sweating increases.

Bronchi dilate.

Heart accelerates rate of beating, increases strength of contraction.

Digestive tract decreases peristalsis.

Adrenal glands stimulate adrenaline secretion, increasing blood sugar, blood pressure, and heart rate.

Liver releases sugar into the bloodstream.

Secretions of the pancreas decrease.

Urinary bladder relaxes.

Urinary sphincter closes.

Blood vessels in skin, skeletal muscles, brain, and viscera constrict. Blood vessels in external genitalia dilate.

Skin and body hair produce "goose pimples."

Secretion of digestive fluids decreases.

Anal sphincter closes.

Insel, Paul and Walton Roth. *Core Concepts in Health*. Palo Alto, Calif.: Mayfield Publishing Co., 1979.

Elijah spared no punches. The Lord listened and then told Elijah exactly what to do.

Step Three: Realize you can't cope with stress entirely on your own strength. But through God, you have a source of unequaled help. Take the problem to the Lord in prayer, and do the following Scripture study.

1. Job 13:15—Put faith in God even when it seems he doesn't care.
2. Philippians 4:4-8, 13—Think uplifting thoughts.
3. Ephesians 3:16-19—Know Christ's love.
4. 1 Thessalonians 5:21—Hold on to the good in your life.
5. Isaiah 26:3—Seek peace.
6. Mark 11:23—Believe the Lord can help you.

The mind of sinful man is death, but the mind controlled by the Spirit is life and peace (Romans 8:6, NIV).

HOW STRESS AFFECTS YOUR JOB PERFORMANCE

Not only can stress lead to the diseases of dis-stress, behavior characteristic of stress could very well lead to the loss of your job. Watch for these signals and take action before such behavior causes you career problems!

Frequent absenteeism—You seem to be finding more and more reasons to miss work. You wish to avoid work-related problems.

Poor time management—You feel victimized by time and sense a loss of control over your personal and work routine.

Procrastination—Normally, you hit the door working, but recently you've fallen into a pattern of putting things off.

Defensiveness—You've begun denying problems exist and are suspicious of fellow employees.

Not up to par—The quality of your work has fallen dramatically. You aren't the person you used to be.

HOW NOT TO SOLVE STRESS-RELATED PROBLEMS

Eating—Some people head for the refrigerator or candy machine when stress hits. Don't—you'll only get fat.

Drinking—Alcohol is often used to cover up stress. Keep in mind that if it does do that, you still pay a high price with your liver and stomach. It's easier to face your problems with all your faculties intact, too.

Smoking—If you think smoking will "soothe your nerves," think again. Nicotine is a stimulant. Besides, it puts you in greater risk of future lung cancer.

Caffeine—Drinking coffee all day is common during periods of stress. However, caffeine has been associated with nervousness, insomnia, ulcers, and headaches. Not to mention the recent evidence which links it to cancer.

die,
    Will you please load
and start the dishwasher?
I love you — see
you tonight.
                Jayne

TO:

He dis

I love you
mother

Heather

INTER-FAMILY COMMUNICATION

FIVE

Keeping in Touch

I often think the most difficult part of being a working mother is the feeling of isolation from one's children. Living in a large metropolitan area can tend to exaggerate this feeling. Every morning, my husband leaves for a city thirty miles to the west; I leave for a city thirty miles to the east; and our daughter goes across town to her school—each one of us is in a different town all day long. So often, I am struck with the thought that I haven't the vaguest idea what's going on in my family's world—particularly my daughter's. What if she needs me? For though I've instructed her teacher time and again to feel free to call me at work, I know she wouldn't want to call for something trivial.

Touch is important to children. But because we working mothers can't reach out and actually stroke our youngsters during the day, we need to discover other ways to give them a sense of security and well-being.

One way to do this is through note writing. We write a lot of notes in my family. Periodically, I'll put a note in my daughter's lunch kit. Sometimes it's a short confirmation of love.

Dear Heather,
  You're my daughter, and I love you.
              —Mama

Another time I may clip a puzzle from the newspaper and suggest that she complete it after school. And at still other times, I may put together a praise letter, glorifying some small act of goodness Heather has performed.

Heather looks forward to these lunchtime notes. They are her contact with Mama in the middle of a long, hard day. For that reason alone, notes are important. But they may also be an effective way to elicit cooperation in household chores. If Heather and her father are going to get home before me, I often leave a note explaining that I expect the living area to be tidied or the dinner started. Somehow, a written note seems more official than a hurriedly spoken request. Of course, it's a nice touch to leave instructions for a fun activity every once in a while. I sometimes suggest in a note that Heather play a board game with a neighbor or make herself a banana sandwich. The spontaneity of these notes makes them more valuable.

Note writing is also a good way to keep close tabs on your child's school progress. When Heather entered the first grade, she would invariably come forward with an arm full of papers just as I was about to start supper, load the washing machine, or straighten the living area. The result was usually a hurried, "Why, that's wonderful, dear."

Then one day I hit upon the idea of taking her papers with me to work and regrading them according to my own scale. Heather was delighted. And so was I, when I sat down at break to a cup of coffee and the wonder of my child's expanding knowledge. On each paper I wrote a note—good idea, I like these colors, great work, and so on.

This plan met with such enthusiasm from Heather that it is now the regular procedure at our house for parental feedback on schoolwork.

Communicating with older children creates an even greater challenge, for each year you'll find less and less information being revealed to you through conversation. This is true even when Mom doesn't work, but the problem is compounded when she doesn't get home before 6:00 or 7:00 P.M. For one thing, children are most likely to talk about their day immediately after getting home. By the time a working mom arrives on the scene, homework, television, and maybe even neighborhood activity take precedence over that which happened several hours ago. Then, too, older children often sense how tired and hurried their working mother is, and decide that it's wiser not to get underfoot.

So, one of the best ways for us to find out what's going on in the lives of these children is to ask questions—open-ended ones that require more than a yes or no answer. Examples: "What did you do in math today?" "What kind of questions were on your English test?" "What are you studying in history?" But remember—when your child begins to talk—be ready to listen! Actually stop what you're doing and make eye contact. Then, accept what is said, even though you may not like what you hear.

Since most teenagers like talking on the telephone, this could be a very effective way to establish conversational rapport with your older child. Try calling home each afternoon during your break for a quick chat. But avoid leaving the impression of "checking up" or calling to give orders.

When you must give instructions *in absentia*, do so in an interesting, nonoffensive manner. For instance, a cartoon related to a controversial family rule, taped in a prominent place, may seem more friendly than a verbal reminder to obey the rule.

To get the conversation flowing back to you, introduce the "talk box." Place a decorated shoe box with a slit in the top in a busy traffic area. Invite your children to write everything from grievances to grocery needs on a slip of paper and insert it in the box. Permission slips, report cards, and other school notes can also be put in the box. After checking the box each night, you should be up on your household's daily affairs.

If older teens balk at the "talk box" approach, you may prefer to instigate a doodle pad. In the book *Get It All Done and Still Be Human* by Tony and Robbie Fanning, one woman said she taped a sheet of blank newsprint to the entire top of a telephone desk and placed a can of colored markers on the desk. Messages, reminders, ideas, gripes, and unusual doodles soon filled up the page—at which time she merely replaced the old with a new. One of the sheets was so interesting and typified the family's life-style so well that she had it framed and hung over the desk.

Another woman has found early morning the best time for making contact with her teenage son. She likes to eat breakfast with him and then continue their visit as she drives him to school. This is a nice way of ensuring your child a good start each day. But if neither of you is a morning person, you can reserve Saturday mornings for a late breakfast at an inexpensive coffee shop. If there is more than one older child in the family, alternate between taking all the children and taking one at a time.

Families who are able to come together each night, but not necessarily at dinner time, might like to try the after-dinner dessert plan. Instead of offering dessert at the end of the meal, serve a dessert in the middle of the evening as a homework/family-time break.

But probably one of the very best ways to communicate within the family is the family council. This solution for coming together as a family works with any number or age of children and can even be effective when parents are divorced—provided communication channels are still open.

Just what is a family council? It is simply a regularly scheduled meeting during which all members of the family meet and discuss anything they like. Each member is encouraged to present his opinion. And while parents should not allow children to carry out suggestions which would endanger their health or welfare, in these meetings, a child's opinion is as important as Mom's or Dad's. For example, maybe a child would like to have a slumber party, but Mom feels the child is too young. A discussion during family council might result in a compromise, allowing the child to invite one friend to sleep over.

Other topics usually discussed in a family council include recreation, disagreements, family rules, finances, and the sharing of household duties. A meeting is not, however, to become an ordinary gripe session.

There are several advantages to the family council. Not only does it lift the burden of decision making off a single parent, it eliminates arguing during the week—everyone knows that the opportunity to discuss the problem will come at its appointed time and that decisions will be made fairly and sensitively. Then, too, children learn within the council

that their views and feelings are important to the entire family—that each person is a valued part of a whole.

WHAT TO DO TO START YOUR FAMILY COUNCIL

1. Discuss the theory of a council with your family.
2. Agree to a place and time of meeting.
3. Decide on a chairperson democratically.
4. Discuss rules for the family council.
5. Select a secretary to record discussions and decisions.

Make the meetings fun. You might, for instance, illustrate the problem under discussion with a simple cartoon drawn on poster board. Then, ask the children what they would do if they were in the cartoon. Another time you might ask family members to write their solutions to a problem on paper and submit them to the chairperson anonymously. Perhaps an opinion poll taken during the week by your secretary could be a useful tool in making a decision. Or, you may want to introduce role-playing as a means of discovering new insights. There are so many exciting, creative opportunities in these meetings. One suggestion, however: do begin with a prayer and end with special refreshments.

No one should be required to attend family council, but attendance is encouraged by the fact that decisions can be made about absent members. If you encourage an atmosphere of openness and fluidity, however, your council will be cheerfully and eagerly anticipated.

Sometimes the communication void in a two-career family is between husband and wife. How does one improve or even maintain a successful relationship when there is so little time for togetherness?

One couple says the telephone is their lifeline. "My husband travels," the wife relates. "Telephoning each other regularly and being open about plans has helped us reach a good level of sharing even when apart."

Attending each other's company functions is also an aid in maintaining communication. Knowing the people your spouse works with will make work-related conversations more meaningful and fun.

Writing notes can also work wonders between spouses. A note slipped into a briefcase which says, "I'll be praying about the 2 P.M. sales meeting" can be just the boost your spouse needs.

Occasionally, there will be problems or concerns in your family that need yours and your husband's full attention. Don't cheat yourself out of a full discussion with a few terse words in front of the television. Schedule a time and place to meet at day's end to work through such problems without the interference of household demands.

DO YOU KNOW HOW TO LISTEN?

Some children just don't share their thoughts, or perhaps they're like my daughter and do so days or months after the fact. A typical mother's response is, "But why didn't you tell me sooner?"

The fact is, very often they have and we were just too busy to listen. Learning to listen in such a way that encourages conversation isn't difficult—it simply requires a concentrated effort.

Dr. Joseph Novello gives some good pointers on listening in his book *Bringing Up Kids American Style.* He says, if you find yourself often monopolizing conversation, stop and ask yourself who owns the conversation. The answer is, the first person who spoke. If it was the other person, your duty is to help him express himself until he indicates a new topic or throws the conversation back to you. If you interrupt with a new topic, you're guilty of robbing the other person of the conversation and his self-esteem.

As you listen, determine the theme, feeling, and tone. Particularly with children, it's not always clear. Listen not just for *what* is said, but *how* it is said. Then keep the conversation going by asking questions, tilting your head in an attentive manner, or nodding with understanding. It's equally important to look at the person, to read body language, and to show through yours that you care about what is being said.

Finally, help close the conversation in a positive way by saying, "Thanks for sharing," or "It was nice talking with you."

Finally, create special events to celebrate the joy of being husband and wife. Candlelight dinners, late evening walks, stargazing on the front porch, and praying together before bedtime are just a few of the rituals which can bring couples together at the end of a very busy day.

By wisdom a house is built, and through understanding it is established (Proverbs 24:3, NIV).

FROM MY JOURNAL

*It's a typical morning—
starting with me re-
setting the alarm for
another fifteen minutes.
Once up, I shampoo my
hair, slip into a dress,
and proceed into the
kitchen where I make
coffee and burn the first
batch of toast.*

*Heather wakes crying.
She doesn't want to go to
school today. She hates
the dress I've laid out for
her, detests the slacks
offered as an alternative,
and would rather die
than wear the yellow
overalls. After telling me
how mean I am to make
her attend dance class,
she plops down in front
of the television to watch
cartoons.*

*As I gather up coats
and mittens and remind
everyone to take their
lunch, Heather an-
nounces that she really
will eat the egg I offered
thirty minutes ago.*

MORNING MANAGEMENT:

SIX

Rise and Shine

I don't like to admit it, but mornings like the one just described can be completely transformed by setting the alarm a little earlier and then actually getting up when it rings. Furthermore, it's been my experience that mothers should rise at least one full hour before their family. If you're like me and need special inspiration to do so, look to Bible women for models.

My favorite example of early risers is in Mark 16:2. Even in their sorrow, Mary Magdalene, Salome, and the mother of Jesus went to the sepulcher at the rising sun. Their reward? Being the first people to discover the resurrection. Of course, our rising isn't likely to match the excitement of that particular sunrise, but Jesus is there to meet you and me in the early morning also. Take a few moments to enjoy his presence. You'll find meditation much easier in the quiet of the new day. But aside from gaining inner spiritual joy, there is another good reason for rising early. We can get more accomplished and face our work with greater peace of mind when our day begins with order.

If you have trouble rising as early as you'd like, read on. These ideas may help you get off to a better start.

1. Plan ahead. Decide in the evening what you'd like to accomplish the next day. Like a business executive, you may even want to make a list. As you sleep, your subconscious mind will actually prepare you for the activities ahead.
2. Develop an evening routine.
   a. Insist upon all baths being taken before going to bed.
   b. Lay out the next day's clothing (this includes yours, your husband's, and the children's).
   c. Pick up the house.
   d. Write special notes to teachers.
   e. Pack school lunches and store in refrigerator.
3. Place the alarm clock across the room from your bed, so you will have to get up to turn it off. Keep a warm robe and slippers close by, however, so that you won't be tempted to return to the warmth of the bed.
4. Splash cool water or astringent on your face for a quick wake-up.
5. Establish a morning routine. Dress, eat a light breakfast, and spend at least fifteen minutes in prayer. This done, open the curtains to let in the sunshine, or turn on the lights to create a warm, cheerful atmosphere. Wake the children and your husband. As they are dressing, prepare a simple but nutritious breakfast. Spend a few minutes sharing in their day's plans. Then, if there's still time, make your bed.

I suppose anyone could be responsible for seeing that the family gets off to the right kind of start each day. But the point is, *someone* has to take the responsibility. If no one else in the family has slipped into this role, a Christian woman can surely see the importance of taking on the job herself. As a mother, you *can* set the tone of the day and ensure that your family leaves a happy, love-filled home each morning. Certainly this is the kind of atmosphere your family is most likely to want to return to at the end of each day.

And in the morning, then ye shall see the glory of the Lord (Exodus 16:7, KJV).

QUICK AND EASY BREAKFAST IDEAS

Hint: After washing dinner dishes, set the table for tomorrow's breakfast.
Serve:

- Breakfast sandwiches: split an English muffin, add a fried egg and a slice of ham and cheese. Heat in oven until cheese melts.
- Cheese toast, fruit, and milk.
- Frozen pancakes, waffles, or French toast, and fruit juice.
- Cinnamon toast, fruit, and milk.
- Cold cereal, toast, and fruit juice.
- Milkshakes.

BANANA MILKSHAKE

1 cup milk
1 banana
½ tsp. vanilla extract
Mash banana, add milk, and blend in blender on high. (You can also blend with a hand beater or shake in a jar.) Serve at once.

If you own a microwave oven, don't forget to use it to prepare scrambled or poached eggs now and then. Though doctors no longer stress the "egg a day," and we're all looking out for cholesterol levels, we do know that high protein foods seem to help school children perform better on tests. Working mothers don't always have time to prepare eggs, but if you know your child is facing a series of important tests, you may want to rise earlier to prepare eggs. Another alternative would be stopping at a fast food restaurant on the way to school and work.

COPING WITH MORNING EMERGENCIES

A Mother's Law of Probability:
If Something Can Go Wrong—It Will Happen in the Morning While You're Trying to Get to Work

Mornings are naturally a bit frantic for working moms—there's such a lot to do in so very little time. But what about those days when things are more hectic than usual—when something over which you have no control seems predestined to keep you from getting to work—period? Because situations like this are every working mother's nightmare, you'll feel more secure if you're just the slightest bit prepared for these mini-disasters. Follow this chart to get a jump on morning emergencies.

EMERGENCY
The baby-sitter calls in sick.

EMERGENCY ACTION
Your options: 1. Stay at home and miss a day of work.
2. Call someone from your alternate baby-sitter list.
3. Make an arrangement with your husband in which each of you takes a half-day child care responsibility. (Bosses always appreciate this kind of effort.)

PREVENTIVE ACTION
Prepare a list of emergency baby-sitters. Your alternatives could include a drop-in service at a commercial day-care center, a call to a relative, or perhaps a stay-at-home mother who would be willing to baby-sit in emergency situations. Talk to each of these people ahead of time so that you can be certain of their availability.

EMERGENCY
Your child is sick.

EMERGENCY ACTION
If at all possible, stay at home. Being sick is stressful enough without the administrations of a stranger or the trauma of being carted across town to Grandma's house. However, if there's a crucial reason for your not missing work, you can again share "home" duty with your husband. Some cities have the unique service of home baby-sitting for sick children. However, these services are usually expensive and best suited

for the professional woman who simply mustn't take time
away from the office.

EMERGENCY
You awake to no electricity.

EMERGENCY ACTION
Grab a flashlight and check the circuit box. If this doesn't
bring results, telephone the electric company to find out if
the problem is area-wide and how long you should expect to
be without power. While speaking with the electric company's
representative, you might ask for the time—particularly if
your household is run by an electric clock. Since you may
have overslept, make a note to telephone your boss of your
probable late arrival.

You won't have use of your hair dryer, and assuming the
power failure is throughout the neighborhood, you can't run
next door. So, don't wash your hair. Instead, pat a cotton ball
soaked in witch hazel on your scalp. Then brush baby powder
or corn starch through your hair. A pretty comb or headband
will complete your emergency hairstyle.

Feed your family a cold cereal breakfast, and depending
upon the amount of time you expect your power will be off,
consider carrying your frozen goods to a friend's house for
the day.

PREVENTIVE ACTION
Select a hairstyle that is either short enough to air dry on
occasion, or long enough to pin up. Keep witch hazel and
baby powder in the bathroom cabinet. If there are frequent
power failures in your area, purchase a hand-wound alarm
clock and a large ice chest for storage of frozen goods. Other
helpful measures include keeping a flashlight near your bed,
and candles and matches in the kitchen.

EMERGENCY
You awake to no water.

EMERGENCY ACTION
If there are very young children in the family, you may have to
consider missing the first half of your work day. In that case,

you need to telephone your boss to inform him of your crisis. Next, contact the water department. Chances are, repair work is being done in your area, and you'll have water again in a few hours. In the meantime, you need to locate a water supply. If you have a baby for whom you need water to prepare formula or other food, you'll need to carry some containers to the nearest gas station and bring some water home.

PREVENTIVE ACTION
Keep a bottle of drinking water in the refrigerator, and try to keep a few cans of prepared formula on hand for feeding the baby in emergency situations.

EMERGENCY
Your car won't start.

EMERGENCY ACTION
If it looks like it's the car's battery, call your husband, who may already be at work, a friend, a relative, or as a last resort, a service station that makes service calls. Then notify your boss that you'll be late. In the event that the problem can't be quickly corrected, and you simply must be at work for an important meeting, call a cab.

Once at work, you can use the telephone to make further arrangements for your car's repair. Someone in your office will probably even be willing to give you a ride home.

PREVENTIVE ACTION
Join an auto club that makes service calls—especially if your husband travels and you're on your own most of the week. It's also a good idea to locate a reliable private mechanic. You'll find the private garage owner more willing to work around your schedule than a large chain-operated one. (Your area's Christian "Yellow Pages" can help you locate such a service.)

In addition, keep a pair of jumper cables in your car trunk, and the phone numbers of all potential helpers in your personal telephone directory. If change is a problem, it's a wise idea to keep taxi money in a special emergency kitty.

EMERGENCY
At the last minute you notice your hem's out, and you have to meet with the company president, first thing.

EMERGENCY ACTION
Staple or tape your hem in place. Once back at your desk, repair with the sewing kit which you keep in your drawer.

EMERGENCY
You're out of toothpaste and mouthwash.

EMERGENCY ACTION
Brush your teeth with baking soda. Rinse mouth well with water.

EMERGENCY
You've broken a nail and can't find a nail file.

EMERGENCY ACTION
Use the striking portion of a matchbook to smooth the broken edge of your nail.

EMERGENCY
A personal problem causes you to cry just before leaving for work. Your eyes are swollen and red.

EMERGENCY ACTION
Soak tea bags in cold water, place on eyes, and rest for a few minutes. Then, with your finger, apply cream coverstick around eyes and nose. Cover area with pressed powder and press a wrung-out damp tissue over face to freshen makeup.

EMERGENCY
You're only days away from making a presentation—and a big blemish appears on your face.

EMERGENCY ACTION
Rub a styptic pencil (used on razor cuts) on the pimple three times a day. It will quickly dry up.

EMERGENCY
You've run your last pair of pantyhose.

EMERGENCY ACTION
Cut the damaged leg off pantyhose and match it with another one-legged pair. At your first free moment at work, exchange your makeshift stockings for the emergency pair you keep in your desk drawer.

EMERGENCY
The children announce they haven't any clean socks.

EMERGENCY ACTION
Turn their cleanest pair inside out, and promise yourself that in the future you will check on these things before going to bed.

EMERGENCY
Your hair is responding to the weather in frizzy, flyaway fashion.

EMERGENCY ACTION
Rub a fabric-softener sheet through your hair for a taming effect.

FROM MY JOURNAL

I am sitting at a typewriter in the college newsroom when two chubby little hands place themselves upon my desk.

"Can I tell you something?" a small voice asks.

"Not now," I answer. The words are flowing for once and I dare not stop. But from the corner of my eye I can see the voice belongs to a beautiful, dark-haired child.

"Wait until I'm finished," I urge. "I'll be through here in just a minute."

The child takes a deep breath and begins what seems a never-ending torrent of words. I listen at length, making plans to give her my full attention after work. But when at last I have finished the story, my visitor is gone—leaving behind a potted plant minus its flowers and a filing cabinet stripped of its labels.

"So who was the little girl?" I ask around the newsroom.

"Oh, that was _____'s daughter," a colleague replied, referring to a former student now employed by a local newspaper.

But, of course . . . I should have known. For only the child of a writer could have talked so animatedly to the rhythm of typewriter keys, seen the potential for nosegays in a begonia plant, and played for hours on end with a handful of index labels.

I like all children, but the off-spring of writers are by far my favorite. They're so colorful and imaginative; so resourceful and persistent. But, then, I suppose they have to be—living with a writer is said to be the pits. Growing up under one must be horrendous!

ORGANIZATION

SEVEN

Setting Things Straight

Regardless of their trade, I've found professional women to have this in common: Our work makes us whole—a fact we've come to know and accept. It also takes an immense toll on our family—in ways we *neither* know nor accept.

Let's face it. If we choose to combine a career with home-making, our lives cannot realistically run as smoothly or calmly as those of traditional homemakers. But one way to minimize the adverse effects of a double calling is to be supremely organized.

Organized people have a clear perception of their environment, have surrounded themselves with tools for effective living, and know how to find these tools when needed. Today's world is so cluttered with fragmentation—doesn't it make sense for the responsible Christian woman to put some order into her data bank of resources?

RESOLVED: I will make my own and my family's life more orderly.

But everything should be done in a fitting and orderly way (1 Corinthians 14:40, NIV).

A NOTEBOOK—WOMAN'S BEST FRIEND

First step: Find a notebook, preferably an attractive fabric or leather one that you plan to keep. Make sure it will fit into your purse, but is large enough to write in. From henceforth, it should be with you at all times.

What should go into your notebook? Anything that comes to you throughout the day. Laundry tickets, birthday presents, recipes, prayer requests, and so on. This is your personal data bank. Use your notebook to plan ahead. Before going to bed, decide what you hope to accomplish the next day and write it in your notebook. Most important, don't just write in your notebook—remember periodically to browse through it! Check on your progress by marking off duties accomplished.

Think you'll join me in my efforts toward attaining order? Congratulations! You have just become a coordinator of life.

HELPFUL HINTS

1. Schedule everything—even the fun things such as eating out and family birthday parties.
2. Keep a spare set of car keys in a safe place so that if you happen to misplace yours, you can look for them at leisure.
3. Patronize shops such as cleaners and repair shops near your home or place of business.
4. Hang a big calendar in the kitchen. Fill in all appointments, birthdays, and other scheduled events.
5. Learn to say "no" without forgetting when to say "yes."
6. Establish a family communication center for leaving notes.
7. Give yourself some peace and quiet time.
8. Develop a reading file. When a magazine arrives via the mail, spend a short time tearing out articles you want to read; discard the rest. Put the articles in a folder that you can carry with you and read during "waiting" moments. Put interesting but not urgent reading into a trip folder—designated for reading on your next trip. Throw away the articles or pass them on to a friend after you've read them.
9. Make a habit of writing dates on things as you put them away. This includes business cards, notes, and clippings.
10. Don't save junk. Sell it in a garage sale or give it to the

children to play with for a while—then throw it out!

11. When reading correspondence, underline in red ink questions you'll need to answer by return mail.

MAKE A LIST

Lists are a key to organization. Don't stop with a grocery list; incorporate this type of planning into every area of your life.
Here are a few lists you may want to start keeping.

1. A shopping list—Keep this ongoing list in your purse or on your kitchen counter. Add to it the minute you think of something you'll need from the grocery on your next stop.
2. A menu list—Make this before going to the grocery store. After shopping, tape it to one of your kitchen cabinets so there'll be no confusion as to "what's for dinner."
3. A gift list—As they come to you, jot down appropriate gift ideas for various family members. When Christmas or birthdays arrive, you'll have only to check your list for that perfect gift!
4. A Christmas card list—And while you're at it, why not a regular correspondence list?
5. A prayer list—Write your prayer requests out and cross them out as each one is met.
6. A book list—Keep a record of books you'd like to read. You'll find trips to the library more profitable when you know what type of book you're looking for.
7. A "to do" list—Before going to bed at night, plan for the day ahead. List the things you'd like to accomplish the next day. Mark the jobs of top priority.
8. A "things I'd like to do" list—On this list you may write anything from eating ice cream to planting rosebushes. When you're going through a blue spell, this list can serve as a true spirit lifter. Make it a point to do something on this list regularly.

KEEPING HOUSE AND A BUSY LIFE TO BOOT

Since you're an active woman, you need to be extra efficient with your housecleaning time. Here are a few ways of effectively managing this responsibility.

1. Hire outside help at least once a month. Yes, it is possible for just about anyone. Teenagers will often work for a reduced rate just to get steady work, while housewives may be willing to clean your home in exchange for another service.

   Between paid housecleaning jobs:
   a. Pick up clutter each evening before going to bed.
   b. Use a feather duster for quick touch-ups in the living area.
   c. Run your dishwasher after you've gone to bed. Put away clean dishes the next day while you prepare the evening meal.
   d. Wash the tub during your bath time.
   e. Keep a bottle of rubbing alcohol in the bathroom. A small amount on a piece of tissue will clean your vanity and sink in seconds.
   f. Clean the refrigerator as you put away groceries.
   g. Train your family to put away or clean up as they go.
   h. Place a basket by the door for gloves, scarves, and hats.
   i. Add a thirty-foot extension cord to your vacuum cleaner, and you'll save yourself the trouble of stopping and starting.
   j. Purchase an extra-long telephone cord or strategically place the kitchen phone so that you can continue cleaning up while talking.
   k. Solve the laundry sorting problem by purchasing dishpans for each member of the family and labeling them with each person's name. Instruct family members to collect and put away their own clothing.

2. Bonnie McCullough, a personal and home management consultant, suggests the simple technique of decluttering the home as an effective housecleaning measure. Based on the theory that clutter creates the illusion of dirt, her procedure involves spending five minutes a day per room for general pickup. Bonnie's advice? Begin where your efforts will show the most. Pick up large items such as cushions first, and work your way down to the smaller items that can be placed in a basket as you go.

3. Ever wonder how to get the family to help with housekeeping chores? Begin thinking of yourself as a working family, not just a working mother.

Your children stand to benefit in many ways from your work. Author David Melton *(Survival Kit for Parents of Teenagers)* believes the benefits of your working should be explained to your teenager in detail. Perhaps it would do just as well to extend his suggestion to all family members. Children need to know that braces, a nice wardrobe, cheerleader fees, or the new bicycle are available partly *because* Mom works.

Melton suggests discussing these benefits at a family meal and then explaining the duties of each person in order for the working situation to succeed—laundry, simple dinner preparation, and so on. He says to give your child a realistic allowance that's worth working for. Then, for each job not completed, dock that person a predetermined amount. Naturally, this requires some secretarial duty and minimal supervision on your part; but the results of a family working together will be worth your efforts.

Giving even small children daily household tasks is important because it's one way that children learn to feel a part of the family. Don't worry if they're too young to complete the whole job. You can be helped by their doing just a part of the job.

One way to gain eager help from your young helpers is to give them important-sounding titles. The person in charge of cleaning bathrooms becomes "Washroom Attendant." Whoever is in charge of picking up living room clutter is the "Main Room Manager," and so on.

Of course, you want to avoid giving your children mindless chores without considering their interests and abilities. (And their abilities do change rapidly as they grow!) Imagine my surprise when I left the ironing board for just a few minutes and returned to find my daughter proudly displaying the garment she had very satisfactorily ironed. She had discovered a new skill which she obviously enjoyed, so I quickly took her off pickup duty and put her in charge of those 100 percent cottons that take so much time to iron.

Likewise, a teenage boy would be delighted to have actual responsibility for washing the car, changing the oil, and filling up the gas tank. And an older daughter shouldn't always get stuck with cleaning up the dinner dishes. Give her special responsibilities as well. She could, for instance, be asked to assist little sister in her school clothes shopping. The idea is to make some responsibilities an honor, so that children will be more likely to participate in family life.

But a word of caution. Since your children's abilities may exceed your wildest expectations, don't be tempted to overdo. Remember, even your teens are still your older *children*.

Be careful not to overburden them with chores. Special consideration should always be made for homework overloads, after-school activities and jobs, or just plain goofing off now and then. You'll recognize your family's happy medium by remembering that the quality of your children's lives should not suffer because you work, but rather be enhanced.

A GOOD IDEA!
Set up a job chart for the family. List all the chores that have to be done. Divide the chart into those jobs which need to be done alone and those which require a team effort. Ask family members to sign up for the jobs they want.*

---

*The Home & School Institute. *Families Learning Together.* New York: Wallaby Books, 1980.

CLOSE TABS ON FAMILY RECORDS

When was the last time you couldn't find an important paper that you knew you had put away very carefully? A personal data system will put an end to such dilemmas and keep your home office organized besides!

If you don't have room for a small two-drawer filing cabinet, purchase accordion folders or a storage chest that fits under the bed; or substitute with sturdy cardboard boxes of appropriate size.

Use the following checklist to remind yourself what to keep and what to discard.

Active File

Tax receipts	Unpaid bills
Paid bill receipts	Current bank statements
Current canceled checks	Income tax working papers

Health benefit information
Insurance policies
Family health records
Receipts of items under
    warranty
Receipts of items not yet
    paid for

Credit card information
Copies of wills
Appliance manuals and
    warranties
Education information
Loan payment books
Loan statements

Items to Discard

Salary statements
Other records no longer
    needed

Expired warranties
Coupons after expiration
    date

Safe Deposit Box

Birth certificates
Marriage certificates
Divorce decrees
Death certificates
Titles to automobiles
Veterans' papers
Contracts

Citizenship papers
Adoption papers
Wills
Deeds
Household inventory
Bonds and stock certificates

ESCAPING THE TELEPHONE TRAP

Many women are disorganized simply because they've fallen
victim to telephone abuse. The telephone can absolutely
wreck our daily living pattern if we don't place restrictions on
its use in our life.

   If friends call you from early in the morning until late at
night, install an answering machine to free you from these
untimely intrusions. When your chores are completed, you
can then return the calls at your leisure. Other helpful hints:

1.   Smile into the phone. When talking on the telephone,
     people have the tendency to mirror the personality of the
     other person. So be friendly, offer a cheerful, wide-awake
     greeting. Speak clearly, listen attentively. And don't carry
     on a conversation with someone else (such as a child)
     near the phone.

2. If talking extends over a longer time than you'd like, here
    are some graceful ways to end a conversation:
    "I know you're busy, so I'll let you go."
    "Listen, I'm going to have to let you go."
    "Can I call you back? I'm expecting a call."
    "Can we continue this conversation sometime later?
    Maybe over lunch?"

But do use your judgment. There's nothing more painful
than really needing to talk to someone, only to be told that
the person "doesn't have time." God will give us a million
opportunities to minister on the telephone—let's be ready to
truly make the most of them!

FROM MY JOURNAL
My husband's on vacation—I'm not. You can imagine the conflict therein. The problem is, I feel left out . . . put upon . . . maybe even a little sorry for myself. But for good reason!

At the end of my long, hard day at the office, I come home to find the family buried in at least three feet of clutter and moving to the jingle-jangle of late afternoon television shows. There's no sign of supper on the table, a stack of laundry sits right where I left it in the morning, and everyone clusters about me in jubilant anticipation of my next move. Is it selfish of me to want my own vacation one of these days?

FINDING PRIVATE TIME

EIGHT

Getting Away from It All

All of us at some time or another relish the idea of getting away—as if moving the body to another location would be restful in itself. The irony of this thinking is that when we return, we face the same pressures and problems that we so eagerly left behind. True rest isn't in moving the body from one place to another. Nor is it in the absence of thinking.

The dictionary definition of "vacation" can give new insights to this often misinterpreted word. A vacation, says Webster, is time free for something else; specifically, time for contemplation. Certainly this is what most of us could use: time to discover ourselves; time to seek the kingdom of God; time for renewal. The marvelous thing about this kind of vacation is that we needn't have time off from our regular work schedule or a stashed away bundle of money in order to take advantage of it! I call such a vacation a *state-of-mind holiday*. Here are the rules of the game:

For two weeks, find vacation time for yourself in your everyday routine—one hour per day. Take on a particular project during this special hour, being careful not to exceed the allotted time period. Suggestions are given below, but follow your own instincts. You'll find a state-of-mind holiday both invigorating and stimulating.

FINDING UNITY WITH GOD

What's required: A love of God; a desire to be at one with him.

Benefits: A change of thought; a refreshed spirit.

Plan two weeks of simple menus with easy cleanup features such as paper plates. (Make certain your family knows it's only temporary.) This should give you an extra hour in the evening. While the children are playing or watching television, find yourself a quiet nook—preferably an area with a door you can close. Now delve into Bible study and prayer.

Choose a particular area of interest—forgiveness, temptation, grief. Check out special concordances and study aids from your church or public library; purchase a Bible study book; or keep a spiritual diary. The sense of calmness and inspiration that you discover during a spiritual vacation won't end with the closing of your books, but will follow you throughout your resumption of routine chores.

"MIND" COLLECTING

What's required: A keen sense of observation; a reliable memory.

Benefits: The joy of being able to return to a scene many times.

Photography companies tell us to capture a moment on film, but there's really a much better way to cherish and keep the precious. I call this kind of savoring *"mind" collecting.* Its beauty lies in the fact that it doesn't require fancy equipment and is always available for the spontaneous joys of life. What better way to spend a vacation than taking mind pictures of a well-loved subject!

Choose any topic of interest—roses, chapels, trees, smiles, and so on. Then, for two weeks, implant these scenes or objects in your mind as you confront them. Record these "mind" scenes in a journal. You may be surprised to discover how much like poetry your descriptions will read.

A VARIATION: BEACHCOMBING

For two weeks try to seek nothing but God. Look for him in moments of gentleness, innocence, goodwill, lighthearted-ness, joy, and kindness.

Again, keep a journal. Decorate it with drawings, tracings, or magazine pictures of ocean-related objects—sea shells, pebbles, driftwood, etc.

HOME WORKSHOP

What's required: A spirit of creativity.

Benefits: Tangible rewards—completed projects.

Is there a hobby or pastime you never have time for these days? If so, the workshop holiday is a perfect solution, and one hour every evening or early morning for two weeks should enable you to get a pretty good start on a project—maybe even complete it! Go for simplicity—the small needlework piece instead of a large complicated one; the writing of fun limericks instead of deep, philosophical poetry. Four such vacations throughout the year could give you four handsome Christmas gifts for some very special people.

Is there something you'd like to learn? Studying isn't just for scholars. Become your own expert. Spend an hour every day for two weeks pursuing your special interest. Write a research paper on the topic. (Hand-bound and decorated copies would make interesting gifts.)

AROUND THE TOWN IN FOURTEEN DAYS

What's required: Untamed curiosity; an appreciation for the past and present.

Benefits: Greater knowledge of your local surroundings; civic pride.

This two-week vacation begins at work on your lunch break and is an interesting way to become acquainted with your community or do those things for which you've never made time.

Prepare for your journey by scanning city brochures and newspapers for places you've never been that are within reasonable distance of your office. Then make a list. Perhaps you'll eat lunch at that tiny Mexican cafe you've always wondered about. Maybe you'll visit a vintage clothing store and purchase something nostalgically romantic. Could be you'll walk to City Hall or rest your feet beside a "downtown" fountain. The key is to shed inhibitions and explore. And remember, whatever you select to do must be brand new!

When the weekend arrives, you can be generous and share this part of your vacation with the family. Go fishing at a forest preserve, do a little local sightseeing, or visit the library and dig up local history.

PRECIOUS MOMENTS

There's no question that a state-of-mind holiday leaves one feeling renewed. But an occasional effort at finding time for yourself is not really enough to ensure a balanced life-style. Relaxing or thinking on a regular basis is an important human need. "Selftime" may even be one way of easing stress. This time is different from pleasant moments with family and friends—"selftime" is the setting aside of hours from both work and relationships.

Yet working mothers often claim such time is nonexistent, or at least not available on a regular basis.

"I've *tried* to set aside time for painting," said one woman, "but every time I manage a few moments to myself, the girls come up with an emergency for me to take care of."

As she spoke, her female listeners nodded in recognition of the problem. There are only so many hours in a day. But a closer look at our personal schedules will actually reveal all kinds of wonderful opportunities for private moments *within* our already hectic routine. We find such moments through proper utilization of "found" time, making better use of existing, untapped time. Sound impossible—certain you haven't a spare second in your already too-crowded day? Look again. Though none of us will find it in exactly the same places, all of us can find some of this valuable time for rest and revitalization by simply using our imagination.

Get started today—find your hidden moments of privacy by exploring a few of these ideas—all tried and tested by busy women like you.

■ Ride the bus instead of driving your own car to work. A friend tells me that "it does take more time, but it's *my* time. I read the newspaper, work crossword puzzles, and sometimes even pray."

If public transportation to your job isn't available, you can claim the same quiet time by joining a car pool.

■ Take advantage of "waiting" time. Whether seated in the crowded waiting room of your doctor's office or in the plush reception area of a Fortune 500 company, you can collect valuable moments for personal use while waiting. Some things you can do in this situation are: prepare shopping lists, write letters to relatives, catch up on your reading of business periodicals, etc. A former boss of mine never left the house—not even for an evening with hubby—without a book under her arm or tucked into her purse.

"It makes me anxious to have to sit in the car while he fills the tank with gas or drops by the office for a quick check," she says. "But if I have something to read, sitting in the car by myself somehow becomes *my* time, and I love it!"

■ Use lunch hour as a breather instead of a noisy social hour. Some ways to do this are:

1. Close your office door, dim the lights, and kick off your shoes. Sit at your desk and practice deep breathing for twenty minutes.
2. Walk to a nearby park and enjoy a picnic for one . . . or just walk around the block for a quick energy recharger.
3. Spend forty minutes browsing in the public library— you can't beat it for a quiet, restful atmosphere.
4. Go home for a change of scenery.
5. Walk through a nearby art museum.

■ Make the ride home work for you—not against you. Listen to soothing Christian or classical tapes on your car's tape player. (If you don't have a tape player but drive long distances each day, consider installing one as a form of mental health insurance.)

■ Take two vacation days and enjoy a four-day weekend. Hire a baby-sitter and do what *you* want to do.

1. Hunt for clothing bargains.
2. Share a long lunch with someone dear.
3. Check into a beauty spa for the "works."

■ Take a half-day off and go home to rest. Actually lie down on your bed with a cool compress on your forehead. When five o'clock arrives, pick up the children from their child-care facility as usual.

■ Make a "Do Not Disturb" sign for your bedroom door and teach your children to respect it. Set aside a part of your day when you won't be interrupted and place the sign on your doorknob during this time. Read your favorite magazines or get into a new novel.

■ Allow your children to watch one or two early evening television shows. Make yourself a glass of herb tea and sit on the patio while dinner cooks.

■ Lock yourself in the bathroom and take a really long bath. Listen to motivational tapes via a battery-run tape player, give yourself a facial, or paint your nails.

■ Take a bike ride. If you need an excuse, let the supermarket be your destination.

■ Relax for twenty minutes on a homemade slantboard. Place your ironing board on the fireplace hearth and re-cline upon it. The inverted position allows gravity to work for you. As blood is brought to the head, the extra nourish-ment and oxygen will leave you feeling rested and peaceful.

■ Go for a walk in the rain. If temperature permits, don't cover up with rain gear. The rain will give your complexion a natural, healthy glow—you'll look as relaxed as you feel.

TIRED OR BORED?

Sometimes we think we're tired when we're really just bored. Fatigue and that worn-out feeling are often caused by unproductive mental attitudes. Reflect on the personalities of people you like to be around. Chances are, they're individuals who take responsibility for making their lives interesting and worthwhile. Here are some tips on putting the "zip" back into your life or merely keeping it there.

Make an effort to really listen to everyone you encounter during the day. Even if they don't have anything terribly interesting to say, your sincere interest in these people may make their day more meaningful. When you look at it that way, can you afford to do less?

Act enthusiastic even when you aren't. Acting so will eventually lead to the real thing. Besides, it's contagious and helps get the job done.

Keep learning—and not just within your job. Learn to do things which give you satisfaction away from your career identity. . . . Take up weaving, plant an herb garden, etc.

Make certain you have something to look forward to each weekend. Plan on eating out Friday night, or take the children to the zoo on Saturday. It doesn't have to be anything elaborate—just a simple deviation from normal routine will recharge your energy and interest in life.

A Menu of Mind Resters . . .

Listen to records
Daydream for a specified time
Sit in a garden
Ride a horse
Sew a simple pattern
Work on your family photo album
Make a rag doll
Create a potpourri

. . . the times of refreshing shall come from the presence of the Lord (Acts 3:19, KJV).

AVOIDING THE POST-VACATION BLUES

Have you ever returned from a wonderful vacation and suddenly been hit with a case of the blues? A vacation of the mind can leave you just as wilted as a real trip away from home if you don't prepare for coming back. Here are a few ideas that work well for returning after any kind of vacation.

1. Make certain your house is picked up before you retreat for your holiday. It will be much more pleasant to rejoin the family if chores are completed and your household is in order.
2. Make a list of things that must be done after the two-week vacation. Put it in a prominent place. Just having it there will take the worry out of not doing something you feel you should be doing.
3. Don't leave your holiday cold turkey. Pamper yourself for a few days afterward with dinner out after work, or perhaps with the purchase of a good novel.

FROM MY JOURNAL
*Every year the student
wives' auxiliary sponsors
a bake sale, displaying
their tempting, calorie-
laden wares in the
medical school's student
lounge. I hate selling
anything, but have
relented this time in the
name of charity. As I
take my place behind a
table covered with gooey
Hello Dollies, a young
white-coated man
surveys our goods. We
hold up the brownies,
the homemade fudge,
the freshly baked lemon
squares—surely he can't
miss the Hello Dollies.
But there is an uncom-
fortable hush throughout
the room. He wants
banana bread. Banana
bread? Bran muffins?
Wheat cookies? We shake
our heads in embar-
rassed shame. There is
nothing on our table
that vaguely resembles
good nutrition.*

*And out of the ground
made the Lord God to
grow every tree that is
pleasant to the sight,
and good for food.*
(Genesis 2:9, KJV).

NUTRITION

NINE

What's for Dinner?

It was dinnertime. Mary placed her briefcase on the kitchen counter and handed her husband the sack of hamburgers.

"I've got to change clothes," she greeted him apologetically.

Once in the bathroom, she slipped into jeans, splashed cool water on her face, and listened to the clamor of three preschoolers discovering the aroma of fresh hamburgers. How well she could visualize the scene—the tearing of papers, the grabbing for french fries, and the crying for ketchup.

"But everyone likes hamburgers," Mary reasoned to herself. "We used to think they were treats when I was a kid."

So why did she feel guilty? What was so wrong with dinner these days that she'd rather stay in the bathroom than join the family? Mary didn't really need an answer—she knew. This was the third hamburger meal she'd served her family over a ten-day span.

"I must be the worst mother in the world," she thought as a tear trickled down her face.

But she isn't—we all know that. Though three hamburgers in ten days may seem to be overdoing it a bit, when it comes to tempting the palates of preschoolers and answering the need for dinner—we understand completely.

If there is one area of life in which American women suffer universal twinges of guilt—dinnertime would win hands down. It's an area of particular concern for Christian working mothers who feel their "table" should be an example to other families in the community. And rightfully so. Long gone are the days when "taking care of our bodies" meant only not drinking and smoking. Today's Christian mother has the additional responsibility of teaching her children about exercise and proper nutrition. But how to do this at the end of a working day is another matter entirely.

Part of the problem may be that many of us set standards for dinner which are no longer applicable in today's world. It has, for instance, taken many years for me to accept the fact that after-work dinners can never be comparable to the evening meals which I enjoyed as a child. Growing up as a missionary kid in pre-industrial Nigeria, I was accustomed to long, peaceful dinners of spectacular dishes served by white-coated servants. After dessert, my parents rose from the table and took us children for a walk on the compound. When we returned, the table had been cleared, the dishes washed, and the tilly lantern lit. How can I live up to that?

I can't. Modern life calls for tasty, quickly prepared foods that can be eaten with a minimal amount of pomp and fuss. Consequently, I've given up the notion that dinner has to be a certain type of food served in a particular way. My present goal is simply to present the most nutritious meal possible in the most cheerful manner. On some days, this might, indeed, be a hamburger from a fast-food restaurant; but on others it may be steamed vegetables and fresh fruits. The point is—as long as we are striving to feed our family with love *and* care, dinner can be a celebration of family life, no matter what the menu or environment.

PUTTING IT ON THE TABLE

Through the years, I've found planning to be the key to happy, nutritious week-night dinners. For me, it all begins on Friday lunch hour when I make out the upcoming week's menus. I ask myself how many meals I need to plan for, and later that night I check foods on hand for leftover possibilities. Then I make a food list for shopping. During the week I've checked the newspaper for specials and clipped coupons for foods that we normally use.

Working mothers don't have a wide choice of shopping hours. We can go at the end of a work day and possibly spend more because we're tired and hungry, or we can go on Saturday or Sunday. Saturday mornings are usually least crowded of the weekend hours, and if your husband's home, you can even sneak away without little ones underfoot.

Every working mother should keep a scrapbook or file box of easy-to-prepare, nutritious meals. If you haven't already begun such a collection, you'll find these recipes in magazines, cookbooks, and by word of mouth. Your criteria for judging such menus: ready availability of ingredients, easy preparation, healthy nutrition, and moderate-to-low calorie content. Sometimes the idea is common enough, but it's having it there in front of you that makes recall quicker and easier. Here are some family favorites to help you get started.*

*Unless otherwise stated, recipes are suitable for serving a family of four.

REUBEN DOGS

For each serving:
1 hot dog in large bun with mustard
1 tablespoon sauerkraut
1 slice American cheese
Heat in 350° oven until cheese melts.

Serve with frozen french fries, tossed salad, and instant pudding.

ENGLISH MUFFIN PIZZA

Split and arrange on baking sheet:
6 English muffins
Combine in bowl:
2 cups tomato sauce
1 teaspoon salt
½ teaspoon pepper

½ *teaspoon oregano*
½ *teaspoon Italian seasoning*
¼ *teaspoon garlic salt*
Coat muffins with tomato mixture.
Sprinkle on:
2 cups grated cheese
Add:
pepper slices
pepperoni slices
mushrooms
Heat in 350° oven until cheese is bubbly.

Serve with green salad and brownies.

STEAMED VEGETABLES—MACARONI AND CHEESE

Prepare any vegetable such as broccoli, cauliflower, turnips, or carrots by cooking in steamer until tender.

Macaroni and Cheese
Cook and drain 1 cup of macaroni according to package directions.
Stir in:
1 tablespoon butter or margarine
¼ *cup milk*
½ *cup shredded cheese*
Sprinkle over top:
¼ *cup buttered bread crumbs*
Bake at 350° for 20 minutes or until crumbs are brown.

Serve with simple dessert of Angel Mana: Butter each slice of angel food cake, top with 1 teaspoon brown sugar, broil until sugar bubbles.

STUFFED BELL PEPPERS FOR SIX

Prepare six peppers by slicing off top and removing seeds. Cook in small amount of water until tender. Drain and set aside.
Cook according to directions:
1 package of Rice-a-Roni Spanish Rice Mixture
Arrange cooked peppers in large baking dish. Spoon Spanish

rice mixture into each pepper. Place extra rice in baking dish between peppers.
Sprinkle:
1/2 cup grated cheese on top
Bake in 350° oven for 15-20 minutes.

Serve with pineapple salad and hot rolls.

Pineapple Salad
For each serving:
1 slice fresh or canned pineapple
Spoon dollop of mayonnaise in center of pineapple ring. Top with grated cheese.

PORK CHOPS CREOLE

4 pork chops 1/2–3/4" thick
1 teaspoon salt
1/4 teaspoon pepper
4 thin onion slices
4 tablespoons uncooked instant rice
1 8-ounce can stewed tomatoes
4 green pepper slices
In a 10-inch skillet, brown chops over medium heat. Sprinkle with salt and pepper. Top each chop with onion slice, pepper ring, 1 tablespoon rice, and 1/4 cup tomatoes. Reduce heat; cover and simmer until tender, about 45 minutes. (Add small amount of water during cooking if necessary.)

Serve with buttered green beans, cottage cheese and peach salad. For dessert: ice cream and cookies.

Cottage Cheese and Peach Salad
Place peach halves on serving dish and spoon cottage cheese into each half. Sprinkle with grated cheese, if desired.

FAMILY CASSEROLE

Cook according to package directions:
1 cup macaroni
Drain and add:
1 can chunk white chicken
1 can cream of chicken soup

Sprinkle top with 1 cup crushed potato chips. Bake in 350° oven for 30 minutes.

Serve with green peas and biscuits.
For evening snack: popcorn.

SUNDAY OR COMPANY DINNER

Chicken and Rice
1½ cups uncooked rice
1 or 2 uncooked, cut up chickens
1 stick melted butter or margarine
1 package dry onion soup mix
1 can cream of chicken soup
3 cups water
Salt and pepper to taste
Place uncooked rice in bottom of large baking dish.
Arrange chicken on top of rice. Salt and pepper chicken. Pour melted butter and cream of chicken soup over chicken and sprinkle onion soup mix over it. Add water. Cover and cook for 2 hours at 350°.

Serve with broccoli and molded applesauce cinnamon Jell-O salad.

Applesauce Cinnamon Jell-O Salad
Prepare large package of cherry Jell-O with 2 cups boiling water. Add 2 cups cinnamon-flavored applesauce. Stir until contents are dissolved. Allow to set in refrigerator until firm (several hours or overnight). May be served as salad or dessert.

QUICK COMPANY DESSERT

Ice Cream Sandwich Sundae
Drizzle ice cream sandwich with chocolate sauce and top with whipped cream.

GARDEN OMELET

Saute in butter or margarine:
1 diced tomato
1 diced onion

1 diced green bell pepper
Set aside.
Beat together 3 eggs per person plus 1 tablespoon water for
each serving. Pour egg mixture into heated frying pan. Cook
without stirring until egg mixture is hard around the edges.
Lift edges and let mixture flow underneath until omelet is
cooked.
Add:
vegetables
1 cup grated cheese
Fold omelet in half and allow cheese to melt. Slide onto warm
plate.

Serve with sliced cantaloupe and hot biscuits.
For dessert serve snack cookies. Simply spread graham
crackers with your favorite canned icing.

SPAGHETTI WITH ZUCCHINI AND GREEN BEANS

3 cups diced zucchini (about ¾ lb.)
1 9-ounce package frozen green beans
1 cup diced onion
1 teaspoon salt
¼ teaspoon pepper
¼ cup oil
1 can tomatoes (16-ounce)
4 tablespoons grated parmesan cheese—divided
½ teaspoon thyme
12 ounces spaghetti, cooked and drained
In large saucepan, saute zucchini, beans, onion, salt and
pepper in oil for 15 minutes or until onion is tender
and zucchini and beans are tender-crisp. Stir in tomatoes,
2 tablespoons parmesan cheese, and thyme. Cook 10 minutes. Toss with hot spaghetti and sprinkle with remaining
parmesan cheese.

Serve with french bread and fruit.

NOODLE DOODLE

1 lb. ground beef
1 can (1 lb. 12 oz.) whole tomatoes

½ teaspoon basil leaves
½ teaspoon oregano leaves
⅛ teaspoon ground pepper
¾ teaspoon salt
4 ounces (2 cups) uncooked macaroni noodles

Brown ground beef in skillet. Drain off fat. Add remaining ingredients. Break up tomatoes with spoon, stir to mix. Bring to boil. Cover tightly, reduce heat to low, and cook for 20 minutes or until noodles are soft.

Serve with a green salad.
For dessert, top partially frozen strawberries with whipped cream.

FRITO PIE

2 cans (16-ounce) chili with beans
2 cups shredded cheddar cheese (reserve ½ cup for topping)
1 medium package corn chips (crumbled; reserve ½ cup
  for topping)
chopped onions to taste
sliced olives to taste

In large casserole, layer ingredients—repeating process until casserole dish is filled. Top with crumbled corn chips and shredded cheese. Heat in 350° oven for 30 minutes or until heated through.

Serve with green salad, Dr. Pepper, and date bars made from a mix.

QUICK AND EASY LUNCHES TO PACK OR EAT AT HOME

SANDWICHES
On a bagel: Tuna salad topped with cheese. Broil until cheese melts.
On whole wheat bread: Egg salad.
On french bread: Salami, provolone cheese, tomato, and onion.
On white bread: Leftover meatloaf.
In a hot dog bun: Canned chili and frankfurter.

SOUP

Carry in an insulated container. Eat with crackers and thick slices of cheese. Take advantage of instant soups which are packaged in disposable cups.

SALAD

Wash greens when you first bring them home from the grocery store. Place in an air-tight container, and you'll be ready to prepare your salad any time. Add tomatoes, cucumbers, onions, etc. Your favorite low-calorie dressing and cottage cheese complete the meal.

HOT MEAL

Serve baked beans on brown bread toast with potato chips and pickles.

When your little ones refuse to eat the planned menu . . .

BANANA BOAT

For each child:

2 slices of whole wheat bread
1 banana
peanut butter to taste

Spread peanut butter on bread, add ½ of sliced banana.

SHOULD YOU OR SHOULDN'T YOU?

During the early months of my new career, I was often frustrated when I arrived home late to find my husband sitting in his chair waiting for *me* to start supper. I mentioned this in conversation to our art director one day, and was surprised at her simple solution to the problem.

"Haven't you learned about frozen pot pies?" she asked. "They may not be everyone's favorite, but when it's late and the family's hungry, why add to the disagreeable atmosphere by arguing over dinner preparations?"

I took the woman's advice to heart and have since made it a habit to keep some type of frozen dinner on hand at all times. And in truth, it works better if the entree *isn't* a family favorite because it's more likely to stay around for a true emergency. On the other hand, frozen foods needn't be considered just an emergency food item. Though usually more expensive than canned goods, frozen foods keep longer than fresh foods, are just as nutritious and a great deal faster to cook in many cases. So, if the budget permits—why not enjoy?

TIPS ON PURCHASING FROZEN FOODS

1. Pick up frozen foods on your way to the checkout counter.
2. Buy only clean, undamaged packages. Report soggy, limp packages to the store's manager.
3. Avoid heavily frosted boxes—they may have been defrosted and refrozen.
4. Make certain that all frozen foods are packed together. Not only do they stay cooler that way, but it will be easier for you to put them quickly away once you are home.
5. In very hot weather, you may find that placing frozen foods in an insulated bag or an ice chest with a thin layer of ice on the bottom will help you arrive home with your food in more stable condition.

SWEET TALK

All well-informed mothers know the merits of nutritious goodies versus empty calories . . . perhaps the real issue is whether or not we practice what we know.

So, don't resort to expensive sugar-coated snacks. Healthy, nutritious snacks will not only give your child (or husband) more energy, but save you money as well.

Kid-tested snack ideas:

- Fresh fruits and vegetables. Skewer fruit or vegetable pieces on a toothpick for mini-kabobs, dip in orange juice, and roll in chopped peanuts. Stuff celery with tuna salad, cream cheese, peanut butter, or cottage cheese.
- Popcorn. Homemade, if you please. And without butter and salt!
- Whole grain crackers spread with herb-seasoned cottage cheese mixed with plain yogurt and grated carrots.

- Pocket salad sandwiches—pocket bread stuffed with mixed vegetable salad. (A spoon of salad dressing is optional.)
- A large dill pickle wrapped in a slice of American cheese.

SPECIAL HINTS FOR MAKING DINNER EASIER ON MOM

1. Stick to simple meals: chef salad, London broil, baked chicken, etc.
2. Learn to clean up as you cook. This will keep you from facing an overwhelming job after dinner.
3. Give your husband a homemade cookbook of fool-proof recipes. Consider assigning cooking days between the two of you. (A teenager can also take a turn.)
4. Post weekly menus on the refrigerator door so the family will know "what's for dinner," and you're spared the annoying question as you walk in from work.
5. Keep an ongoing grocery list of items needed in a conspicuous spot where everyone may add on.
6. If energy permits, cook the night before. For instance, brown and cook a roast for one hour; store in refrigerator. Peel vegetables. Store in plastic container in refrigerator. Next evening, combine ingredients and cook for another hour.
7. Cook double the amount needed. Arrange leftover portions in oven-proof or microwave dishes. Seal with foil and freeze for future use.
8. Consider the benefits of investing in a microwave oven. Quick defrosting, retention of valuable nutrients, and fast meal preparation are considered well worth a series of payments by most working mothers.

WAYS EVEN A WORKING MOTHER CAN IMPROVE HER FAMILY'S DIET

1. Bake, boil, and broil your meats and poultry.
2. Remove skin on poultry to cut down on fat.
3. Steam or microwave your vegetables to preserve nutrients.

4. Serve whole wheat bread.
5. Use lowfat milk.
6. Trim fat off meat before cooking.
7. Try seasoning with spices and herbs instead of salt.
8. Eat raw fruits and vegetables whenever possible.

FROM MY JOURNAL
The wonder is that children ever make it at all. I mean, considering what adults unthinkingly do to them day in and day out, I'm amazed at our children's resiliency to neurosis. What I'm trying to say is that today I called Heather "Fatso." That's right. I called my thin, long-legged, beautiful daughter "Fatso," and in so doing, watched her crumple into the heap of self-contempt that I had known she would. But you have to understand—she was being so naughty! I was combing her hair, and she was berating me in that annoying tone of voice that only a seven-year-old girl can manage. And so I simply couldn't resist the temptation of succumbing to grade-school mentality and "hitting" where I knew it would hurt.

Of course, now I'm the one who hurts. Heather may forget that I called her an unkind name. But I'll never lose the mental image of my small daughter choking down sobs and saying, "Imagine your own mother calling you a 'Fatso.'"

He who guards his lips guards his soul . . .
(Proverbs 13:3, NIV).

CONTROLLING OUR SPEECH

TEN

What Did You Say?

I think the matter of godly speech involves far more than
politely refraining from foul language. To me, it is the mastery
of a constructive, well-groomed vocabulary. I believe what we
say should in some way inspire and uplift the thoughts of
others—but you'd never know it from listening to me! Here
are some of the ways my mouth has gotten me into trouble
and what I've discovered we as Christian women can do
about it.

PUTTING FOOT IN MOUTH

How many times have I contracted the dreaded hoof-in-
mouth disease? More often than I care to admit, I assure you.

"Carla's so childish," I pipe across the room.

"Sh—," everyone hushes me. "She's right over there."

Or how about this one?

"Is that one of your neat bargain buys?" I ask a friend
whose hobby is recycling clothing.

"No, I bought this at Neiman Marcus," she answers,
tight-lipped.

"But I didn't mean . . . I mean you're so terrific at finding
good buys. . . ."

It's too late; my friend has moved on, giving me a hurt,
betrayed look.

We've probably all said the wrong thing at the wrong time. Sometimes we meant exactly what we said even though we knew it was unkind; at other times the statement was simply misunderstood. At any rate, once we have opened our mouths, we are left with the problem of how to get our feet out of them. Here are some suggestions:

1. We can attempt to explain why we said what we did.
2. We can drop the whole issue, hoping it will disappear.
3. We can pray.

Obviously, prayer is the best choice of the three. There is real value in seeking the Lord for comfort and forgiveness, so ask God to help smooth out the situation. Ask him for strength to approach the wounded one to ask forgiveness, too. Then, sit back and see how he has already helped. Sin, though not admirable, reminds us of our mortal state and how desperately we depend upon the Lord for continued growth. And when we are humble enough to confess our sins, we find that embarrassing, uncomfortable incidents can be turned into blessings.

TELLING WHITE LIES

Have you ever been tempted to tell just a "little" lie, believing it preferable to the truth? Most of us have. We may have been faced with whether or not to alert a store clerk who under-charged us, whether or not to withhold information on a business report, or maybe even whether or not to tell our spouse exactly where we were for so long.

I was faced with such a temptation not long ago. Both my husband and I were attending school. But because his school didn't provide student housing, we lived in student facilities offered by my university. All was fine and good until I discovered that I couldn't manage a family, a job, and a full course load. The problem? Student housing was contingent upon the occupant being enrolled in a full course load. When it came time to renew the lease, I faced a dreadful dilemma. Should I buy time and lie (the computer would eventually catch on) or should I tell the truth? I had been raised on the truth. But was this any time to fall back on old-fashioned values?

After much thought, I decided to be honest and admit that I was no longer carrying a full load. And sure enough, scarcely a month had passed before we received an eviction notice. Strangely, however, I wasn't as frightened as I had imagined myself being. I simply went to the student housing office and explained to the manager that without the low rent rates, I couldn't finish school, and I was so close to completion.

The man looked straight through me, as if remembering a similar time in his own life, tore up the eviction notice, and said quietly, "Be out a month after graduation."

Truth is of God. When we submit to telling little lies here and there, I don't think we can claim to be worshiping the Lord. We are, in a way, breaking the first commandment: "Thou shalt have no other gods before me." Choosing truth is following the way of God—what could be more natural and liberating!

USING GOD'S NAME

I am seldom startled by profanity these days, but not long ago an "Oh, my God" turned my head. The overly dramatized statement had come from the mouth of an eight-year-old. It was the opening of my ears to the extensive use of this phrase by many children. And, yes, I'm shocked. I'm shocked that we've allowed such an important, powerful phrase to become a commonplace slang expression among our children and ourselves.

Used in its proper context, "Oh, God" can have mighty implications. It is the doorway to God's love—the two words with which we can always call on him in time of need. I can't even count the times I've called upon the Lord, depending upon him to pull me from despair to joy, from illness to health, and from fear to peace. And I have always gained the immediacy of his love. Calling out to God is a part of our Christian inheritance. When we experience the inner harmony that accompanies our seeking God, his name takes on a heightened significance to us—and we'll not be so likely to spit it out as slang.

COMPLAINING

I once worked in an office where the employees' conversation was made up almost entirely of complaints. These women complained about their children and husbands, their home furnishings, their after-work activities—you name it and they could berate it. One day we were standing around the coffeepot when I began a derogatory narrative on something my family had done. Suddenly I realized it wasn't the first such story I had told during break. I had joined the ranks of the habitual complainers.

Most of us fall into the habit of complaining innocently enough. What with our lives full to the brim with activities, we may begin complaining about our daily comings and goings instead of merely talking about them. We'd like to talk about how well the children are doing in school, but that would be bragging, so instead we complain about the car pool. We'd like to talk about how handsome our husband looked in his new suit; but not wanting to sound like a romantic teenager, we complain instead about the dirty socks he left by his chair. We'd like to exclaim about the rich softness of the grass beneath our feet. But since that would sound eccentric, we complain about the inconvenience of lawn care.

Complaining is a subtle sin. To find out why, read the Scripture passages below. (Note: Complaining is often referred to in the Bible as murmuring.)

Complaining involves:
1. Discontent—Matthew 20:11
2. Disapproval—Luke 5:30
3. Dissension—Acts 6:1
4. Discussion or gossip—John 7:12
5. Disbelief—John 6:41, 43

How do we overcome complaining? Perhaps the answer lies in determination. There is no shortcut to Christian

maturity—only the way of patience and determination.
Remember Philippians 4:4-8, 13, and no matter the situation
or environment, approach life from these angles. Surrender
your life to God. As we live to please God, we'll find we're not
as ready to complain about every little thing. Last of all,
take Psalm 34:1 as a personal motto. Wear it in your heart
and on your face every day.

*I will extol the Lord at all times; his praise will always be on
my lips* (Psalm 34:1, NIV).

WARNING: WORDS CAN BE DANGEROUS—
WATCH HOW YOU COMBINE THEM!

A number of everyday words should be banned from the
dictionary—and certainly from the language of mothers
and children! Some of these words (combined in the most
unkind ways) are:

1. What?
2. I hope you don't get mad, but . . .
3. I hate you.
4. Do I have to?
5. Do something with your hair.
6. Why don't you ever do as I say?
7. All the other kids are . . .
8. I wish I had . . .
9. We'll see.
10. Another time.
11. Do you love me?

WORDS OF ENCOURAGEMENT—
TO BE USED FREQUENTLY AND FREELY

1. Good try.
2. Much better.
3. Hang in there.
4. Terrific!
5. Beautiful!
6. I appreciate your help.

7. Marvelous!
8. It looks like you put a lot of work into this.
9. Very creative!
10. Very interesting.
11. Super!

FROM MY JOURNAL
Grocery shop, then on to Heather's school to pay tuition. There are doughnuts on a tray in the office. Heather does not ask for one, but later talks about how she kept looking at them in hopes of being offered one. I am so proud of her. My daughter is learning manners! When did I ever instruct her on the impoliteness of asking for something not offered? For a moment I have the smug feeling of having done something right, even if I don't know what it was. We go immediately to the bread shop and purchase a big box of Hostess doughnuts.

Therefore, as God's chosen people, holy and dearly loved, clothe yourselves with compassion, kindness, humility, gentleness and patience (Colossians 3:12, NIV).

MODERN ETIQUETTE

ELEVEN

A Little Kindness Never Hurts

It was my generation who threw out the rules of etiquette along with hypocrisy, but I don't think any of us were ever against good manners. When properly exercised, good manners consist of common courtesy—nothing more. And though rules of etiquette are often interpreted as phony "affectations," their real background lies in the art of thoughtful living . . . doing nice things for others, making others feel more comfortable, sympathizing with others' hardships, and rejoicing in their happiness. While this kindness actually glues societies together, it doesn't come naturally to either children or adults.

I don't for a second buy the insincerity of forwardly social people. But I do recognize the fact that boning up on acts of kindness can be one of the greatest success-building steps we and our children take. Here are just a few of the often neglected manners in "my" world that deserve another look from a different perspective.

THE R.S.V.P.

Who needs it and who cares? The customary request for your response to an invitation is seldom thought of as anything more than a bother. In reality, however, the hostess needs to know your intentions in order to plan for her party. You show that you care by giving her the information she needs.

Many people assume one only needs to respond to an invitation if able to attend, but it is courteous to notify your hostess one way or the other, unless directed otherwise. You can respond by telephone or on a folded letter sheet (a letter sheet folded twice to resemble a two-page book). Regrets need no explanation other than you're "sorry but will be unable to attend . . . maybe next time."

Since the art of responding to an invitation seems to be somewhat difficult for adults, I believe in requiring children to answer for themselves as soon as they can talk.

THANK-YOU NOTES

Be generous with your thank-yous. There are a lot of reasons for letting people know we appreciate them or a particular action they're responsible for. Write such notes on 3½" x 5⅛" folded cards. A monogram, name, or crest is generally on the front of these notes; writing goes on the inside.

As for children, introduce them to the art of thank-you notes even before they can write. Encourage them to draw pictures of the received gift as a means of thanking the giver. Though it's certainly admirable to insist that such notes be written the day following a party, don't let a time lapse serve as an excuse for not carrying through with the project. This activity requires a little supervision in the way of nudging— allow your child a good month to complete twenty cards. (The same goes for adults. If you had good intentions to thank someone but seem to have let it go a little beyond the fact, be big enough to thank him/her anyway. Our society is so busy, everyone can understand the belated thank-you.)

HOSTESS GIFT

Any overnight stay other than a slumber party merits a hostess gift. Fancy soap, a book, or a bottle of hand lotion makes a nice thank-you for these occasions. I like to leave a gift on the guestroom dresser with a note on the day of my departure. This custom goes back to my days as a missionary kid when traveling always meant staying overnight in another missionary's home. To verbally offer money for hospitality was unthinkable. But because we were all on limited funds, it was the custom to leave an envelope on the dresser with a small monetary token of appreciation.

When my husband was in graduate school in Minnesota, we all carried the idea of hostess gifts into the dinner realm. Following the European custom, we brought a small gift such as cheese to one another's dinner parties. With all of us on tight student budgets, these thoughtful contributions were always welcomed and often added significantly to the meal.

OTHER HOSTESS GIFT IDEAS:
- A closet sachet
- A board game
- A loaf of home-baked bread
- A poem or limerick about your host

Please don't forget your relatives. Chances are, we impose upon them the most and yet thank them the least!

Of course, giving doesn't always denote material things. A well-mannered guest gives the gift of courtesy by arriving on time, leaving at the appropriate interval, and contributing to the fellowship of the party. Both children and adults need to make a conscious effort to participate in the games planned, eat the food served, listen well, and share in the conversation.

DINNER PARTY HOSTESS TIPS

There's more to a successful dinner party than an expertly cooked meal. Part of the hostess's responsibilities when entertaining in her home is to make certain all of her guests are comfortable throughout the evening. I find most of us are quite adept at filling glasses and finding chairs, but there are at least three things we could all use a little coaching on.

1. Serve dinner within thirty minutes of the time stated on the invitation. Please don't make guests die of starvation before announcing that dinner is served. If an unexpected delay occurs, be thoughtful enough to serve carbohydrates such as fruit juice to tide guests over.

2. Instruct your children to ask to be excused before leaving the table. It is a signal that the "children's hour" is over and may reassure guests that the evening is not going to be spoiled with the constant interruptions of children.
3. When women friends offer to help with the dishes—kindly refuse. Nor should you attempt to wash dishes on your own. Stack them in the kitchen and enjoy your guests.

AUTO ETIQUETTE

With as much time as people spend in the car these days, we really should practice a certain amount of consideration when others join us in our auto excursions. If, for instance, you're offering someone a ride in your vehicle, be kind enough to clean the car before calling on your passenger guest. There's nothing more uncomfortable to a guest than easing her best-dressed self into a car seat sprinkled with our children's cracker crumbs. Other pointers:

- Adult passengers should be offered the front seat; children should likewise offer their friends the back window seats.
- Children should be taught not to stand in the back of the car and breathe down adults' necks. In fact, if everyone is properly strapped in with seat belts, this bad habit is impossible. It is also the law in some states that children must be secured in the car. Loud talking, eating, and fighting should also be discouraged when in the car.
- And there is another aspect of car courtesy that few of us practice—driver courtesy. (I'm sorry to say that women seem to be the worst offenders.) Allow an occasional car to pull in front of you during a traffic jam . . . one car ahead of you won't make that much difference in your arrival time. And don't forget to nod a friendly "thank you" when others offer you this courtesy.

INTRODUCTIONS

When it comes to introductions, very few of us feel adequate. I believe this is because introductions as a social courtesy have been grossly overlooked in the training of middle-class

America. How many times have you stood by uncomfortably while your friend carried on a conversation with someone whom you not only didn't know, but weren't even introduced to? Even worse is the realization that we've put people through this misery ourselves.

I still can't claim success in the area of introductions, but it's helped a great deal to follow the advice of a fellow businesswoman: Stop worrying about making a mess of things and go on with the introduction. What does it matter who is supposed to be introduced first? When we make a sincere effort to help others fit into the group, our efforts never go unappreciated.

WHEN NAME CALLING ISN'T SO BAD

People may not like their given name, but try calling them by the wrong name or forgetting their name altogether and you've just made a very unpleasant impression. On the other side of the coin, watch the pleased reaction of people when you greet them using their name.

If remembering names isn't your thing, it should be. Each person's name is a unique and wonderful part of him. God knows our name.

I have called you by name; you are mine (Isaiah 43:1, NIV).

Knowing people by name is important if for no other reason than as a way to help others experience the feeling of human worth. Realizing this, we as Christian women should never be content with a flippant, "I'm terrible at names."

When we can't remember names, we simply haven't learned them in the first place. We never *heard* them. I was faced recently with this situation when a new employee came into our department at work. I "forgot" her name three times in a row. Of course, in truth, I had arrived at work preoccupied with what I needed to accomplish. So, every time the woman's name was given to me, my mind raced over it to what I really wanted to think about. I solved the problem by writing her name down on a piece of paper. Interestingly enough, I never had to refer back to my note—the act of writing the name had caused me to focus on it long enough to plant it in my memory.

Experts have a long list of hints for remembering names. The next time you meet up with a new face you may want to try one of these tips to help you remember the name that goes with it.

1. Catch the name; study the face; make up a crazy combination of the two.
2. Nail the name by association. Think of a person with the same name; or make up a silly rhyme using the name.
3. Anchor the face in your memory. Notice the person's features, coloring, posture, and voice.
4. Write the name down at your earliest convenience. Keep a supply of small cards in your purse, excuse yourself to go to the restroom, or sneak off to an out-of-the-way corner and record names with associations.
5. Be sure you heard the name correctly in the first place. If you're not sure you caught it properly, ask that it be repeated. Say the name aloud; ask how it is spelled.

EXTENDING WOMANLY WARMTH

There's a peculiar thing about being shy. People don't accept it. Those of us who suffer the pains of timidity find it hard to believe anyone would actually hold us responsible for not speaking first; for not initiating introductions; for not reaching out and holding and touching. But the fact is, people do hold us accountable . . . and it isn't unusual to have our timidity mistakenly labeled as aloofness.

At the other end of the spectrum are those lucky outgoing people who are never afraid to speak up and reach out. And yet, when it comes to genuine warmth, these people quite frequently fall short themselves. Always in the mainstream of life, they often simply forget to show their love and concern for others.

Christian women can't afford to leave other people out. To do so is in direct opposition to what our faith is all about. But very few of us have been prepared for the role of "fishers of men." We gladly accept what others have to offer us in the way of friendship; but when it comes to extending love and concern beyond our secure little world—we're at a sad loss.

The Bible gives us many examples of women who exemplified warmth and kindliness in everyday life. Rebekah, for instance, was chosen as Isaac's wife solely because she possessed these traits. (Read Genesis 24.) Abraham's servant asked God to direct him to Isaac's future bride by letting her be the woman who not only offered *him* a drink of water, but his camels as well. "By this I will know that you have shown kindness to my master" (Genesis 24:14, NIV).

A woman in the New Testament won Jesus' respect when she lovingly anointed his head with costly perfume. (Read Matthew 26:6-13.) Talk about stepping out on a limb! Jesus could have reacted in any number of ways (and the disciples did!). Fortunately, Jesus said, "She has done a beautiful thing to me" (Matthew 26:10, NIV).

Still later, Lydia's invitation for Paul and his companions to visit in her home was recorded in the book of Acts. (Read Acts 16:11-15.) Paul says of the invitation, "And she persuaded us" (Acts 16:15, NIV)—a statement which indicates Lydia's invitation must have come across as warm and sincere.

There is nothing in the Bible to suggest that any of these women had vivacious, outgoing personalities. In fact, we know that Rebekah and Lydia were interacting with complete strangers—so merely speaking at all must have been difficult under the customs of the time. But at any rate, all three women took the risk of possible rejection and offered their friendship before it was asked for. And in each case, the step forward was appreciated.

Great women aren't made overnight. But that's all right. Even those of us who have a severe inability to show warmth can become the loving women we want to be. If we want people to know that we like them and care about them, we don't have to hope that they "feel" it. We have only to demonstrate behavior that says as much. So often *what* we feel and how our feelings are interpreted are completely opposite.

This doesn't mean we have to undergo a personality change at this late date. (Experts would tell us that's nigh to impossible anyway.) What we can change, however, is the way we react to life's situations. Since reacting is a learned response, with patience and practice, we can actually learn how to respond to common experiences so that people can properly interpret our feelings.

Personally speaking, the inability to extend a feeling of warmth to other people is probably one of my greatest hurdles. It seems my heart always feels one thing, while my body language betrays me with movements that say another. So, here are a few actions I've learned in order to show people the "real" me. This is not to say I'm always successful at it. For me, learning to react so that I can be properly understood has been a slow, painful process of unlearning thirty years of standing back and waiting for the other person to act first. But most of the time, these little tricks do their work by showing someone I care, and that I'm including that person in my world.

TO SHOW PEOPLE THEY'RE INCLUDED

1. Smile.
2. Move over to make room.
3. Use a warm tone of voice.
4. Walk over and lead the person to your group.

TO BUILD SOMEONE UP

1. Clap for the person.
2. Take hold of his/her hand.
3. Make a complimentary A/OK sign.
4. Do a little back slapping.

TO SHOW PEOPLE THEIR FEELINGS ARE IMPORTANT

1. Become aware of which subjects people may feel emotional about.
2. Listen to determine another person's feelings or background related to the emotional subject.
3. Listen to put yourself in another's place.

4. Make a real effort to offer silence to someone.
5. Reveal yourself to others. People welcome personal insights.

None of us is everything we'd like to be for others. But with a little practice and effort we will soon be quite adept at the Christian art of thoughtful living.

God himself is teaching you to love one another (1 Thessalonians 4:9b, TLB).

FROM MY JOURNAL

It's Sunday afternoon. Heather and I are putting away groceries when a packet of macaroni stirs up nostalgic happenings of the past.

"Remember how it was before you went to work?" my daughter asks. "Remember how after we bought groceries, you'd make us macaroni and cheese and we'd sit in front of the television watching your show?"

"Um, hum," I murmur.

"Oh, that was so much fun. I wish we could do that now," Heather adds.

"Me, too," I answer truthfully.

But a few days later, Heather's words come back to me with a haunting reality. Of all the good—really good— things I've done for my child, she chooses the watching of soap operas to cherish as memories of our happy-together times. The incident tells me that it doesn't really matter so much what we do with our children, but just that we're there— beside them doing something and bringing them happiness.

RICH FAMILY TIMES

TWELVE

Give a Good Day

Can you remember:

> Red M & Ms
> *My Weekly Reader*
> Dodge ball
> Roy Rogers
> Recess
> Coke floats
>   and
> Spaghetti-strapped sundresses?

So can I. But I also remember making jelly tarts out of Mother's dough scraps and playing tiddly-winks on the floor with Daddy. Which brings to mind the question: What will my child remember twenty years from now—day school and yogurt pops? Perhaps.

But there is another possibility. What if Christian parents pull together and create real homes with loving and caring at the center of the hearth? Instead of wishing our children "a good day" as they leave for school or other activity, why not strive to see that they do indeed have a good day? Why not *give* them a good day?

Sharing the goodness of life is one of the very best ways to spread the love of God throughout our children's lives. Take note that we are not striving to give a material blessing in this instance, but rather we are seeking to share that which will result in an improved mental and spiritual state. Giving in this way is highly enriching to the benefactor as well as the recipient.

A busy journalist discovered how to give her three children the gift of a continued sense of good things to come, by preparing personalized gift certificates. Propped up in bed one night, she made a list of all of her children's favorite things that she seldom had time to supervise . . . a pizza picnic, blueberry muffins, charades and popcorn, etc. Then, using ordinary index cards and colored pens, she wrote out certificates for each child. One child received a certificate for a visit to the fire station, another received a certificate to go to a high-school basketball game, and the third received a certificate worth sixty minutes of playing kickball with Mother.

You don't have to make certificates for special moments, but the system may help commit you to some of the larger projects. Smaller activities can be spontaneous—though you may want to consult your list every now and then. Here are a few ideas for Mom or Dad to build from.

1. Look at clouds
2. Snap fresh beans
3. Watch the sunrise
4. Fly a kite
5. Make ice cream
6. Jump in a pile of leaves
7. Drink a cup of cocoa
8. Eat by candlelight
9. Play a board game
10. Go horseback riding
11. Hold hands
12. Take the stairs instead of an elevator
13. Take the elevator instead of the escalator
14. Take a hike
15. Build a fire
16. Go roller skating
17. Clean out a closet

18. Pop popcorn
19. Barbeque
20. Dance crazy dances
21. Make muffins
22. Make a picture book
23. Write to the President
24. Start a leaf collection
25. Go from morning until lunch using only one hand
26. Draw a map of the community
27. Collect and press wild flowers
28. Roast marshmallows on an open fire

Another important point of contact to make with your child is to let him see you in your office environment. Make arrangements with your boss to bring him in for half a day. (Christmas is a good time to do this because everyone's feeling kind and benevolent and work schedules usually aren't as tight.) Since your child should be old enough not to disturb others when you attempt this activity, you can give him a new coloring book and crayons or some quiet game suited to his age and let him entertain himself as you go about your work.

There are other fun activities which belong to everyone—both children and parents. These are special family activities which require the cooperation and enthusiasm of each family member for true success.

Post news of upcoming family times on a bulletin board or refrigerator. Your children will soon be watching this "information center" with excited anticipation.

Of course, there is always the obvious—a picnic, a community play, the circus. Don't underestimate the fun behind ordinary events. (I can still remember the thrill of *every* picnic we went on when I was a child.) Besides, you can always add a surprise angle. For instance, one woman packed individual box suppers for her family in decorated gift boxes. Another idea is to have an indoor picnic on a dreary, rainy day. Be as "corny" as you like—it's one of the privileges of belonging to a family.

Other ideas:

- Introduce a family game night. Play *Clue, Monopoly, Scrabble,* and so on. Serve Coke floats for a special snack.
- Take a ball to the nearest swimming pool and play catch.
- Create Christian comics. Cut comic strips from the daily or Sunday newspaper. White out the dialogue with Liquid Paper. Have your family change the story to demonstrate Christ's love for us.
- Give each family member the opportunity to tell a joke at the dinner table.
- Schedule a checkers championship. Each family member plays one game with every other family member. Keep track of the winners. The person with the best win-loss record is the champ.
- Build a family collage. It should contain small objects that have had emotional meaning for each member of the family during the year. Programs, school papers, tickets, etc., are good items to start with.
- Create a housemark or family monogram. Using the family name, a housemark is similar to a personal monogram. Example: The last name plus the first initial of each family member. The housemark is selected by the whole family. From there, encourage family members to stencil the design onto personal property. Dad or an older child could even carve the housemark above a door frame.
- Begin a family journal. Purchase an attractive "blank" book and explain to the family that everyone is invited to contribute to its contents. Place it in a visible spot along with a pen. Descriptions of great family moments, news clippings, poetry, and personal insights on family situations are all viable contributions.
- Build a family vegetable garden. Allow each family member to be in charge of one vegetable of his choice.
- Have a "treat the family like company" night. Prepare a special dinner, set the table with your best dishes, candles, and a centerpiece. Naturally, everyone comes to the table not necessarily dressed up, but at least pleasantly groomed.

■ Plan a "do something nice for someone else" night. As
a family unit, select someone who could use some cheering
up. It could be a shut-in church member, a new child on
the block, or a special relative who's down and out. Now
let each family member decide what he can give. Though
everyone's abilities will be different, here are a few suggestions.

>   Write a poem.
>   Paint a picture.
>   Sing a song.
>   Tell a funny story.
>   Make a flower arrangement.
>   Bake cookies.
>   Write a letter.

■ Give a grocery party. Everyone in the family gets to select
one item at the grocery store (unbeknownst to each other)
for a meal. The surprising mix can make for a hilarious,
fun-filled evening.

■ Designate a family worship hour. If you can't realistically
gather more than once a week, do so then! Something is
better than nothing. Sing songs, follow a family devotional
guide, and pray sentence prayers. During the rest of the
week, remember to pray at mealtimes and to share in
bedtime communication with God.

And the list of things to do with your family could go on
and on and on. . . . Why not pledge to stop and smell the
roses with your family today? As you do, remember to save
some time for just being there and telling each child how
much you love and appreciate him.

*This is the day the Lord has made; let us rejoice and be glad
in it* (Psalm 118:24, NIV).

Going to school:

Heather:
"Mommy, did you know any of the pilgrims?"

Me:
"Are you kidding? That was a little before my time!"

Heather:
"Oh . . . well, do you suppose Daddy did?"

FAMILY HERITAGE

THIRTEEN

Once Upon a Time

I've always felt there is a certain genuineness about people who savor the past. So when Heather tells me she is saving her cuddle blanket for her own children, I'm touched. New, expensive, upbeat, and popular are not always best. Sometimes life's real treasures lie in old things and old ways. It makes me sad to realize that so many of these splendid things are passing away before my generation's very eyes.

I'd like to think my future grandchildren will one day inherit from our culture. I want them to have a good family library, a love for letter writing, an appreciation for reading aloud, and so on. But to do so, I'm going to have to make the commitment to bring these things into Heather's childhood and loosen my own embrace on the "now." Let me tell you about some of my preservation projects. You may want to adopt one or more of them for your own family.

THE HOME LIBRARY
Paul to Timothy:

When you come, be sure to bring the coat I left at Troas with Brother Carpus, and also the books, but especially the parchments (2 Timothy 4:13, TLB).

Communication methods seem to be more exciting by the day, but believe me, nothing will ever replace the feel and smell of a fine book. One of the ways we can make certain our own children experience this pleasure is to provide them with a home library. Developing this resource is actually a simple procedure that can become a pastime within itself.

First, select the site. Though a separate room is probably the "dream" of every earnest reader, you can build your family's library on adequate shelving in any area of the house. This is not, however, describing the typical bookshelf we see in most homes, for to be really useful, your library must be built around a definite plan.

Ask yourself the purpose of your home library. Many families will agree on the need for a basic reference library with recognized works from many categories. Dictionaries, atlases, encyclopedias, how-tos, and even beautiful picture books will be the backbone of such a library. It's nice to have ready access to various subject matter as your children approach them in school studies.

As the children grow older, you may want to develop a specialized working library featuring information behind each family member's special interest. You won't need new books—good, sound, used copies will work nicely. Scarce editions, not in the best of shape, can be rebound later on. Of course, special volumes often make attractive displays in the living area—in which case, you'll want to give more attention to condition.

Have a fair sampling of all kinds of books—new, used, paperbound, and preciously bound. When Heather repeatedly took out the same book in the school library, her teacher suggested that she give other boys and girls an opportunity to read the new title.

Heather replied with a terse, "But all my books at home are so old!"

And she was right—for though she had a larger selection than most children, Heather's books were almost exclusively hand-me-downs from older cousins. With this brought to our attention, Olie and I are now passing these books on to others and remembering to add more variety to additional book purchases.

Also, during the planning stage of your library, it's wise to decide who'll be using it. If, like me, you really enjoy loaning books, you'd better have multiple copies of those favorites—perhaps a hardcover and a paperback edition. That way, you can lend the least expensive copy without fear of losing your treasure. Good books are like blessings—they should be shared; but use your judgment and lend only to reliable people.

Above all, be a discriminating buyer of books. There are so many books on the market and lots of them are not worth the paper they're printed on. Choose carefully! Here are a few guidelines for stocking your library.

1. Browse through the public library. Take note of those books which appeal to you and write down the title and author of each in your notebook.
2. Check the actual use of the book by looking at the library book card, or inquire of the librarian.
3. Ask a schoolteacher what she thinks you ought to have in your home library.
4. Read book reviews in newspapers and magazines.
5. Learn the names of authors you trust and enjoy reading. Look for their works. Find out what books *they* read.

One final word: Only extra money should be spent on building the home library. The joy of a new book is diminished if little ones are hungry or improperly clothed. Besides, there's no need to rush through the building of a library; this is a true-life adventure that can carry you through many years of enjoyment.

LETTER WRITING

Like cold water to a weary soul is good news from a distant land (Proverbs 25:25, NIV).

What can a generation that has practically liquidated the art of letter writing say to their children about it? Mainly that the joy of finding a real, honest-to-goodness letter amid bills and junk mail is immeasurable and gives one such a tremendous feeling of warmth and satisfaction that we hate to see this fine tradition pass by the wayside.

I can remember sitting at the table listening to my mother reading letters from my grandmother. Always colorful accounts of "Smalltown, U.S.A.," her letters were fascinating revelations to us youngsters who had grown up in the African bush. So, in a way, my own love for letter writing is a gift handed down by one who loved me. But gifts are only special if they're utilized, and I'm afraid I haven't always lived up to my family's accepted letter quota. Here are some ideas that have helped me improve my correspondence record while teaching Heather some of the joys that come with writing to a friend.

Try these:

Circle Letter—Traveling from one family member to the next, the circle letter is housed in a shoe box which is filled not only with letters, but with photographs, recipes, original poetry, and other items of interest. Each recipient adds to the box; the last to receive it sends the box back to the original letter writer.

Postcards—Kept in your purse, postcards can be pulled out whenever you're waiting at the doctor's office, bus stop, or wherever. If you purchase blank cards at the post office, they're already stamped, and you need only drop them into the nearest mailbox when you've finished your note.

The Letter File—If you find that when you sit down to write a letter, you can't remember what's happened during the week, the letter file will solve your problem. Throughout the week, put programs from the children's plays, invitations, sales receipts—anything that pertains to something interesting you'd like to share—into a large folder. Keep the folder in your kitchen where you'll be likely to use it.

The Underlining Technique—To answer questions that people ask you in their letters, make it a habit to underline these portions of your mail with a red pen. Put the letter in your letter file; then when it's time to answer your mail, the red underline will bring those important questions quickly to mind.

Pen Pals—Some of my favorite correspondence has been among Christian friends. The following letter is from a woman I met at a convention. Though we visited only briefly, it was enough for us to know that we had much in common. Her letter is a shining example of Christian support.

Dear Jayne,

I was so thrilled when I got your letter saying you had sold your book. I can't wait to read it. I had just been thinking of you right before I received your letter. I feel I got to know you so well for the short time we had together. I would love for us to get to visit again sometime. I haven't really decided whether I will come for the convention or not—but if I do I will probably come alone. If God works things out I will come even though I'll be about seven-and-a-half months pregnant (my big news!). . . .

We've also moved to a new house—just what we prayed for, at a price we could afford. We have a shop for Dennis's work, about an acre of land, and around 3,000 square feet including the basement (great for kids to play in!). The house is stone and about thirty years old but in fairly good shape. There's a lot we need to do to it—buy drapes, fix up the yard, get furniture, paint floors, etc., but it's so homey. If you ever come to Amarillo we have room for you to stay with us (your husband and Heather, too).

As far as writing goes, I know someday I will write something, but right now I am so busy with the children and running a household that most of my writing is letters or just personal diary notes or meditations. I did write a short story that I just haven't gotten ready to send anywhere. It's so inspiring to hear from a writer friend. I may get busy and send it off. I really want a typewriter so I can get my own work in submission shape.

Dennis and I are going to be teaching in a home Bible study together on Monday nights. I'm looking forward to doing this together and the results God's promised. He'll use our bit of abilities and multiply them as he did the loaves and fishes to feed others who are hungry. What talent we have is not nearly as important as the fact that we've given it to the Lord. God uses ordinary people to show forth his extraordinary power and love.

I hope this letter brightens your day and finds you full of joy—if not, give joy to others and it'll be given to you good measure, pressed down, running over! May God bless your husband and Heather.

Love,
Kathie

LOVE GIFTS

Sometimes I'm reminded of all the gifts I should have given, but didn't. Oh, not that there's a lack of gift giving in our family, but I'm always keenly aware of the "gifts" of myself that I didn't seem to have time to share.

"Next year," I promise myself, "I'll do better."

But deep down inside, I wonder: Will I ever have the confidence and willpower to give the gifts I want to give— those wonderful life-sharing gifts that really count?

Then it occurs to me that if I start now, this very day, perhaps I can squeeze at least a portion of these special gifts into a lifetime of giving.

This year, instead of a toy microwave oven, I'll give weekly (or at least monthly) breadmaking lessons to Heather.

My mother baked once a week out of necessity; baked goods were hard to come by in Nigeria during those years. As she pinched together the sides of the last cinnamon roll, tucked a loaf into its snug pan, and brushed the top of a coffee cake with butter, big sis, Barbra, and I clambered up to the cabinet. It was our turn. With Mom's dough, we would fashion a multitude of sweets—danish pastries, napoleons, desserts of all kinds. (Never mind that our only ingredients were dough and strawberry jam!)

By the time I was thirteen, Mother had stopped baking. We were back in the States and she said Pillsbury did a better job anyhow. But it's funny that I should remember the smell of rising yeast and the touch of sticky dough with such pleasure. And it's surprising that even in these modern days there are few activities which give me the sense of accomplishment and satisfaction that bread making does.

Perhaps this is the year to let your children take a more active part in your baking, too. This year, in addition to giving each child his own loaf to knead, allow him to measure the ingredients alongside you. Announce each ingredient out loud so that he may subconsciously memorize the recipe. Helping our children master a bread recipe is presenting them with a practical living skill or "living" life insurance.

The following variation of an English tea bun recipe is an excellent dough recipe for dividing among children, as it bakes in small ovals like miniature loaves and seems to be resistant to over- and under-kneading.

ENGLISH TEA BUNS
4 cups flour
¼ cup shortening
1 teaspoon sugar
1 cake compressed yeast
1¼ cups warm water
2 teaspoons salt
Put the flour through a sieve and rub in the shortening and sugar. Cream yeast in half the liquid, and dissolve the salt in the remainder. Mix into the flour mixture; knead and allow it to rise until double in size. Divide into pieces and make into small ovals about 4 inches across. Brush with milk, put on a greased baking sheet, let rise again, and bake for 20 minutes.
Oven temp.—450°

Then Jesus declared, "I am the bread of life. He who comes to me will never go hungry, and he who believes in me will never be thirsty" (John 6:35, NIV).

Instead of a pottery set, I'll give Heather homemade clay and the freedom of expression.

No wonder there is often an urging within us to make something from clay. Nothing is so wondrously gooey and messy. But equally as thrilling is the finished product itself . . . the satisfaction of bringing order to fragmented disorder. Just watch a child's amazed facial expression as he gazes at his finished clay product. I believe his amazement is the realization that he can create something from very little . . . that he does indeed have dominion over land and beast. This is quite a mind-expanding introduction to creativity that no one should miss. But do pass up the extravagant toy potter's wheel. It can come later when your child has learned what he can do without fancy equipment.

When I was a child, my father sometimes took us to the clay pits. We'd all climb into the mission's old station wagon and drive through a maze of winding bush roads until Daddy recognized a landmark that hid our wonderful playground from the road. Then, single file, the six of us would walk quietly down the small worn path through towering elephant grass. Suddenly, we were standing in an open circle of red—everywhere we looked, the ground was dry, sunbaked clay. What a magnificent sight!

We would gather clay and take it home to be soaked in water and made pliable. Soon we would be laboring over the size, shape, and function of our miniature pots. Perhaps if we had had a potter's wheel, our vases would have been balanced and wouldn't have leaked. But somehow I can't help but think we were better off *for* the lack of fancy equipment. It allowed us an important element in design development—freedom of expression and exploration.

PLAY CLAY
Mix:
2 cups baking soda
1 cup cornstarch
Blend well. Add:
1¼ cups cold water
Mix until smooth.
Heat to boiling, stirring constantly. Boil for 1 minute. Mixture should be the consistency of mashed potatoes. Spoon out onto plate. Cover with damp cloth and cool. Knead lightly and roll out on wax paper. Cut out designs with cookie cutters or shape by hand. Let dry until hard (24 to 48 hours). Paint with tempera or watercolors. Allow paint to dry, then coat with clear shellac or clear nail polish.

From this simple exercise, your child will learn to fashion

ornaments for the Christmas tree, as well as design a unique assortment of jewelry and other items. Years later when he or she is struggling through the lean days of early marriage or student life, knowing this skill can lead to the creation of gifts and attractive things for the home.

Yet, O Lord, you are our Father. We are the clay; you are the potter; we are all the work of your hand (Isaiah 64:8, NIV).

Instead of a talking robot, I'll give Heather thirty minutes of reading aloud each week.

There was once a time when a Viewmaster was really something else! Today, it's almost an antiquated curiosity piece next to the home computer and electronic game boards. Not that Christian women should oppose progress (our children need to master those machines in order to function in society), but I do believe we should feel a definite responsibility toward helping our youngsters cope intelligently with technology.

Technology has a far deeper impact on family life than we may want to realize. Sure, we're aware of the communication problems which television has created for the family. Some of us are even beginning to gain the upper hand and are controlling the TV rather than vice versa. But now we have machines helping our children with homework, playing the role of opponent in games of skill, and researching answers to the questions that once might have been asked of Mom or Dad. Do we really want to turn every aspect of our child's life over to a machine?

Society may point in that direction, but this is one instance in which scientists and rulers don't have the final word. For within every mother lies the power to shape the environment around her into a better place for her children, grandchildren, and great-grandchildren to live in. One way we can be certain that our children inherit our values and beliefs, regardless of the technological state of the world, is through our conscious effort to give word-of-mouth instruction.

Understand that no matter how wonderful computers are, they will always be primarily linear. A computer is best at repetitive, left-brain, logical work. This means it can't stare out windows and dream visions. It can't see reality in new ways, try to give form to the formless, or ask why. And so, mothers may be the integral link in the continuance of right-brain, non-linear, random creation.

It's also important to remember that machines become obsolete, are dependent upon an energy supply and man-made conditions which may or may not always exist. If we allow our children to rely too heavily upon machines for instruction and entertainment, and they in turn do the same with their children—a great deal stands to be lost.

Take religious instruction, for example. The story of God's love is always within one generation of extinction. Our children must know how to pass their Christian heritage on without a dependence upon technology. Audiovisual equipment is certainly a good teaching aid, but unless our children hear the Word of God from us, they may never really know the meaning of what we stand for as Christians.

I am convinced that our children must learn to memorize Scripture—and for two vital reasons. First, it will enhance their worship in years to come. And second, but perhaps even more important, it will give them protection against inner destruction. Think back to the people who claim they wouldn't have endured concentration camps and other persecution had it not been for the Word of God stored in their minds. God forbid that anything so terrible should ever happen to our children, but the point is, we don't know what lies ahead. What we do know is that we're the ones who must equip our children for life.

So I would claim that if we can commit ourselves only to one story time a week, it should be a Bible story. After that, history, classics, and poetry can all be enriching and made more meaningful to our children through our own explanations, learning, memories, and teaching techniques.

I view the precious gift of passing on as essential to the continuation of Christian culture. Sure, there's a lot wrong with today's world. But there's so much more that's right and wonderful—so much that's worth every effort of saving and preserving. And this can be our gift to the future.

These commandments that I give you today are to be upon your hearts. Impress them on your children. Talk about them when you sit at home and when you walk along the road, when you lie down and when you get up (Deuteronomy 6:6, 7, NIV).

FROM MY JOURNAL
*So Heather is in
Washington tonight—
2,000 miles away
visiting Granny and
Grandpa Ray while I sit
here in the living room
listening to the echoes of
her absence. Goodness,
but life seems quiet
without my lively seven-
year-old.*

*"I can't wait to get her
back," I tell Olie.*

*"But, you know, of
course, she'll never be
the same," he teases.*

*I am silent. Because
he's right. Heather will
not ever be the same
child. This trip across
the country will broaden
her whole perception of
life. She'll meet new
people, eat strange
foods, participate in a
variety of different
activities . . . and all
without the crutch of my
own vision. And this is
what makes it worth the
price of a plane ticket
and the lonely days
ahead.*

DEVELOPING RELATIONSHIPS BETWEEN CHILDREN AND ADULTS:

FOURTEEN

Someone Special

Heather's visit to Granny Ray's cost me well over a week's salary and was not something we could easily afford. But for Heather to develop a meaningful relationship with my parents was a major goal of mine—I could scarcely afford not to spend money in this way.

One of the reasons I placed a high value on Heather's visit was that I had grown up far away from my own grandparents. I had never had the opportunity to visit on a one-to-one basis. When my grandfather died at the age of eighty-two, it occurred to me during his eulogy that I had never known him—not even a little bit. "Pop did that?" I kept saying to myself as the events of his life unfolded before the mourners. Right then, I vowed I would do everything possible to help my child become better acquainted with her absentee grand-parents.

En route to this goal, however, I discovered that simply matching one's child up with her grandparents every once in awhile isn't enough. To be really comfortable with this special relative during a summer or other holiday visit, the child must already have experienced the rewards of developing friendships with older people. This can be done by introduc-ing a "significant other" into your child's life.

When my big sister and I were children we were best friends with a single lady who was also our mother's favorite friend. Barbara Epperson never talked down to us, was always pleased to see us, and opened doors of adventure to us that Mother would never have dared. Making cinnamon rolls, digging ant hills, and climbing mountains are just a few of the things I remember Barbara E. sharing with us kids. But most of all, I remember it was Barbara E. who took it for granted that one day I would write professionally. Her belief in me was probably one of the most significant influences on my life. Barbara E. wasn't elderly during this time of influence, but she was an adult in "another" world. Being her friend helped me view people outside of my own generation as very like myself.

Many people aren't open to friendships with older or younger people because they've only experienced friendships within their peer group. Children, being the great imitators they are, will pattern their friendships after Mom and Dad's—and an unfortunate cycle sets in. This is a sad syndrome because older or younger friends can round off the edges of all of our lives, but even more so our children's.

For instance, a child who loves books may have parents who don't. A child who likes to garden may not have access to earth. A child who likes to dabble in paint or putter with tools may belong to a family who never has time for such pursuits. How wonderful if a child can spend time with someone who shares his interests and who will help him develop them.

If you would like your child to have a significant other in his life, you'll need to help him develop the friendship. Try some of the following ideas—being present at first, but willing to step into the background when you sense the relationship has meshed.

Visiting—It doesn't have to be a faraway place. Begin the habit of visiting an interesting friend on a regular basis. This might be every day during warm months when people spend a lot of time in backyard fence rites; or it could be an informal once-a-month agreement. Need an excuse? Fresh vegetables from your garden or a small portion of your own baked goodies are always welcomed.

Listening—During these special visits, teach your child the art of listening by listening attentively yourself to the older friend's reminiscing. Encourage your child to ask questions such as: Do you remember what your grandmother was like? Then, make a concentrated effort to hear the other person's reply.

Taking lessons—There is much that an older person can teach. (Older in this context refers to anyone who is in a different generation than your child.) Perhaps both you and your child could learn to crochet or knit from a friend. Helping our children value those skills which are normally passed on from mother to daughter and not learned from books is a true life-giving gift.

Writing—Write a letter or send a friendship card to your child's significant other. Your child may want to draw a picture of a flower or his pet.

There are endless ways to help our children form friendships outside their own little realm of experience. And it doesn't really matter how we go about it, as long as we remain loving and sensitive to the people and the situation. We may even discover that our own relationship with the "grandparents" has become deeper and more meaningful in the process.

FROM MY JOURNAL
Kindergarten Days

Mrs. Hudson tells me she is having discipline problems with Heather. Heather, she says, is loud, aggressive, and unkind to her peers.

I am taken off guard and can only think to apologize. But once home, I tear the situation into a thousand tiny pieces. How much of it is Heather's fault? How much Mrs. Hudson's? How much mine?

Finally, I attack the problem head-on in the same old-fashioned, no-nonsense way my own parents would have done. I question Heather.

"No!" she cries. "I'm going to tell Mrs. Hudson she's wrong. I'm not bad!"

"That's not what I said."

Oh, dear. . . .

First Grade

At Heather's open house, Mrs. Stewart comes up hesitantly. "Mrs. Garrison," she says, "I'd like to have a conference with you sometime."

Then, noticing my discomfort, she adds, "Heather's a leader. She's quick and intelligent. And I love her so much. But she has a problem— she's so very aggressive. . . ."

I nod understandingly. How well I know my child.

Second Grade

Heather has primed me all week.

"Mama, when you go to the art auction, don't forget to look at my puppet that was chosen for the school art show," she says.

And, sure enough, there among the Picasso and Dali prints is my daughter's paper sack puppet. Mrs. Felton rushes over to me.

"Did you see Heather's puppet?" she asks excitedly. "I can't tell you how proud I am of that child—she is a real go-getter."

I wait to hear the inevitable. That my child is aggressive, domineering, etc. But it never comes, and my heart is painting pictures of another kind.

No discipline seems pleasant at the time, but painful. Later on, however, it produces a harvest of righteousness and peace for those who have been trained by it (Hebrews 12:11, NIV).

SCHOOL BEHAVIOR:

FIFTEEN

A Classroom Classic

Heather has spent a lot of time on the bench during recess these past few years. It's her school's most formidable punishment for talking in class, being tardy, and so forth. Part of me doesn't mind that my active child is being reprimanded for her gregarious behavior—I was always so shy, I can't remember ever getting into trouble at school. But, on the other hand, some things are a mother's duty, and upholding school policy is one of them.

"Heather," I say, approaching the subject carefully, "were you the only one who had to sit on the bench?" (There I go again—what does it matter?)

"Oh, no," Heather answers, "everyone had to."

"Everyone?"

"Yeah," Heather answers, "everyone except the ones who didn't have to."

Dealing with bad behavior away from home is no easy feat for parents who weren't there when the supposed improper conduct took place. In all honesty, it's often hard even to picture our children doing some of the things that are reported to us. Still, there is the feeling that we at least ought to *try* to mold their conduct outside of the home into an acceptable expression, even if we aren't there to see the results. And, of course, this has to be done in some way that doesn't impend on the child's sense of self-respect or his feelings about life.

Serious behavior problems call for outside counseling. But if it's ordinary, everyday behavior patterns that we're dealing with, parents can do more to improve the situation than anyone else.

I come from a family that believed in directness. With my parents there was never a question as to how we kids were to behave when away from home—they told us. Furthermore, I've found this system works just as well today as it did back then. Try it. When you receive a report of poor conduct, simply appeal directly to your child. Tell him how you feel and ask that the behavior be stopped. Explain why such behavior is inappropriate, but be ready to show affection. You'll find this approach suitable for all ages and just about any behavior situation. As an added plus, you'll probably be pleasantly surprised at how easy it is.

If this tactic doesn't work, you can always go the incentive route. Promises of future pleasure can be used to start and stop behavior patterns. One year when I was having a particularly hard time getting the point across, my husband and I awarded Heather gold stars for each day of good school conduct. Heather wanted a pair of roller skates, so we decided a hundred stars would earn the skates. It took months. But in the slow process of earning those skates, our daughter mastered self-control in classroom talking.

An older child may be more interested in working toward a certain privilege such as giving a party or being allowed to take on an outside job. And, no, this is not bribery. Look around you at today's premiums, sales incentives, and paychecks—all of life is made up of rewards for jobs well done.

When judging a child's behavior, however, always be sure to look at intent. Very often, what is misconstrued as bad behavior is only the child's inability to cope with a situation. This can be particularly true at school where some children may sincerely need parental help in developing good citizenship habits. Consider the child who doesn't know how to whisper—no wonder he's always being called down. In this instance, why not instigate a whisper day and encourage your

child with a game of all-day whisper practice on the weekend? Likewise, if aggressive action seems to be prominent
school behavior, make a point of helping your child learn to
express himself verbally. Help him see that he doesn't have to
lose his position as a leader just because he's going to be
acting in a less forceful manner.

As in other discipline areas, hunt for good days on which
to praise your child, and ignore a few of the "bad" reports.
Our goal in promoting good classroom conduct is not only to
help the teachers maintain an atmosphere conducive to
learning, but to aid our children in becoming healthy, whole
adults who can function in society at large.

But if classroom behavior problems seem easily solved—
don't sit back and relax yet! Your expectations of good
behavior should carry over into after-school care, summer
camp, visiting at friends' homes, etc.

It has been said that part of disciplining is knowing what
you expect from your children and being comfortable with
those expectations. The problem is that today's parents aren't
too sure where freedom to grow ends and permissiveness
begins. Child care expert Dr. Benjamin Spock says parents
can raise a child well by being too strict or by being too easy-
going. According to him, the trouble occurs when we're strict
out of hostility toward the child or permissive out of guilt.

The guilt factor is big among working mothers. For us,
permissiveness may seem easier. We may let reports of bad
behavior slip by because we feel that, had we been home,
behavior problems would never have occurred. Or perhaps we
learn about the problem at the end of a long day and simply
don't have the energy to grab the bull by the horns.

When one mother received news from her son's summer
camp that he was wrecking the efforts of his counselor, she
was defensive.

"Since he can't stay home during the summer, the least I
can do is be understanding," she said.

But in truth, her kindness was doing more harm than good.

Professor of psychology and pediatrics at New York
Hospital-Cornell Medical Center, Dr. Lee Salk, said in a
recent newspaper article that "permissiveness means no rules
and regulations. But that's not caring," he said. "Children do

not enjoy it, nor do they want a parent who sets no rules or standards of behavior."

So children of all ages do need behavior guidelines for when we're not there to remind them. But what kind of rules and how do we enforce them when we're away from the scene?

Try beginning with just one rule, but insist that it be upheld. Call this rule *respect*. Respect for parents, respect for peers, respect for institutions, and respect for others' property. Here's how the rule works.

Respect for parents. Dolores Curran, author of *Traits of a Healthy Family,* says parents model respect within the family, and that if parents don't insist upon it for themselves— teachers, ministers, policemen, and other authority figures certainly won't receive it either. How right she is!

Respect may mean different things in different families, but in my family it means:

1. Children may not talk back to parents—though heated discussions are permissible.
2. Children may not use language which parents do not approve of or use themselves.
3. Children must ask permission before going to someone's house—even if it's only across the street; and they must telephone to ask to stay longer should that situation arise.

In return:

1. Parents must respect differing opinions.
2. Parents must speak politely to children.
3. Parents must avoid belittling remarks or highlighting the faults of children.
4. When leaving the house, parents should tell children where they are going, even if it's a quick, "I'm off to work now," and should telephone to say they'll be late.

Respect for peers. It's easy to see the interaction of respect between parents and children. The same principle works outside of the home as well. When we encourage our children to treat friends with the same kindness and respect Mom and

Dad expect, they'll find themselves in appreciative company. Children who are required to be sensitive to the feelings of family members will naturally do so outside of the family. They will wait their turn, refrain from bullying, and help out when someone younger or weaker is in a bind.

Respect for institutions. When parents are strong institutional supporters, whether of school, day care, church, or camp, children sense it's not wise to buck the system. Why have Mom *and* the teacher on your case? But at the same time, children need to be secure in the knowledge that if things do go wrong, Mom and Dad won't defend an institution over a child without being absolutely certain of the true situation.

Respect for others' property. From their very early years, children should be taught to handle their friends' toys with the same care they do their own. As they grow older, however, disrespect for others' property can mean anything from writing on desks to stealing candy from the corner store. Whenever a child does show such lack of respect, he will grow only through *acceptance* of consequences. Perhaps you'll insist he wash down the desk or return the candy. Of such painful experiences . . . great people are made.

By now, you've probably discovered that helping our children behave on their own two feet while away from home requires a lot of time and attention from us when they *are* home. Be patient if it seems to take an inordinate amount of time to get the point across. Remember how often you had to remind your toddler to say "thank you" before it became automatic? In matters of discipline, learn to give of yourself in a loving, caring manner, knowing that as you do so, you're helping your child develop the necessary self-discipline for maturity.

FROM MY JOURNAL

"Jayne," Olie called across the telephone wires, "Mom's in the hospital—possible heart attack."

I grab my coat and head for the hospital's waiting room. It's a dreary place—rows of plastic chairs, thumb-worn Reader's Digests *and somebody's desperate attempt at oil painting on every wall. With typical detachment, I turn my attention to the people.*

"How interesting," I find myself thinking. "They're all friends through their fatigue and anxiety."

I watch them clasp one another's hands, jump up to answer each other's phone calls, and lovingly console the unfortunate ones whose fate has been quickly resolved. I listen to them share secrets that wouldn't normally escape family confines. Finally, after what seems like hours, I latch onto the conversation of two women nearby.

"Yes," says the older of the two, "they did determine that he had heartworms and there was simply no hope." Her voice sounds weary, but there is a hint of pride reflected in the tilt of her chin.

The other woman gasps out loud and I sit up straight.

"Can people have heartworms?" I ask. "I've never heard of such a thing!"

The older woman is not amused, but accepts my ignorance gracefully and with forthrightness.

"It was a dog," she says.

GIVING YOURSELF

SIXTEEN

Heart to Heart

It seems the older my husband and I grow, the more frequently we find ourselves in hospital waiting rooms. Aging parents and young children have a way of reminding us that life is precious. What struck me as most disturbing about the episode with Olie's mother, however, is that I remained primarily a spectator throughout the entire ordeal. Like a child, I had entered the waiting room at the designated hour, sat where directed, left with the family to eat, and been careful not to ask questions or give advice in any capacity. Olie and I even followed his parents home when his mother was allowed to leave, where we continued our vigil on the living room sofa. It wasn't until a neighbor walked in with a complete meal for my husband's parents that I realized something was amiss.

"I should be doing that," I said to Olie.

And it was true. But having never viewed myself as completely grown up, it hadn't occurred to me to take charge in this crisis by offering comfort and food. That role had always belonged to someone else—to another generation who did it with skill. The fact that the job was now mine frightened me. I didn't have the slightest idea how to go about doing it!

Women are busier these days—most of us really don't have as much time to attend to the needs of others as our mothers did. And yet, people are still giving birth, still dying, still undergoing operations and all the other events of life that call for a little care-giving. So when our mothers can no longer do the giving, who's going to take over?

One way to become a care-giver in spite of our hectic life-styles is to begin looking for ways of doubling up when friends or family need our attention. A big stew, for instance, could feed another family as well as yours. A trip to the zoo could include the child of a sick mom. A moment of prayer could be shared with a distraught friend. One woman does laundry for friends who need help. This is an excellent idea because it can be done at home—enabling you to go on with your own family's routine. Another way to double up is to do shopping or run errands for someone else while you do your own.

Still more ways a busy woman can help others:

1. Offer to pick up some books for the recuperating person—or bring some of your own that you've already read.
2. Pay for a one-time housecleaning job or help the person in need by checking into available social services. Ill or elderly people often don't have the strength or know-how to get such services started.
3. Tape record church services for those who aren't able to attend.
4. Carry a single rose to a shut-in.
5. Send cards to the sick—daily. Call for a brief chat, when you're sure they're feeling well enough.
6. Take a loaf of fresh french bread and a pound of butter to someone who needs a lift.
7. Instead of flowers, consider giving the hospitalized patient an especially pretty pillowcase. It will pick up spirits by bringing a homelike atmosphere into the unfamiliar hospital room.
8. Remember the family during times of crisis. Perhaps your greatest gift could be giving someone an hour off from bedside sitting.
9. Upon a death in the family, take a can of coffee, and bacon and eggs—instead of the inevitable casserole.

10. Double your cooking efforts and take a complete meal to a family in need by utilizing this simple recipe.

> Multiply amount by number of persons being served.
> Wash and slice thinly:
> *1 potato*
> *1 carrot*
> *1 onion*
> *¼ green pepper*
> *small handful of fresh or frozen green beans*
> Add:
> *several chunks of cheese*
> *salt and pepper*
> Wrap in:
> *2 cabbage leaves*
> Wrap all ingredients in aluminum foil, place on cookie sheet, and bake 30-35 minutes at 375° in the oven.
>
> Hot rolls and instant pudding complete this very simple but delicious meal.

But a word of caution. Don't expect laurels for your efforts—even if that pie you carried to a recuperating friend was the first one you've made in six months! People under stress often exhibit behavioral regression and, like a child, tend to take acts of kindness for granted. No matter—give *yourself* a pat on the back. You've just joined the network of Christian nurturing and have taken your place among mature women. No wonder the glow on your face is from feeling good about yourself!

"Verily I say unto you, Inasmuch as ye have done it unto one of the least of these my brethren, ye have done it unto me" (Matthew 25:40, KJV).

Most of all, it's important to remember that people who have good marriages aren't any smarter, better, or luckier than those who don't. The difference is primarily in the fact that these people simply believe in marriage. Those of us who have been married long enough to beat the national odds may give the impressioin of leading perfect lives and having it all together—but we don't. We, too, have problems with money, boredom, jealousy, and the like. But we believe in marriage to the extent that we work these problems our within the marriage. In this respect, I hope all of us who are happily married will lend support to other married couples. People need to be reassured that in spite of the world's message, divorce isn't the only way to improve one's situation.

With a lot of work and perseverance, we can find ourselves, enjoy happiness, and know true freedom, all within the bounds of matrimony.

"Therefore what God has joined together, let man not separate" (Matthew 19:6, NIV).

FROM MY JOURNAL
*Christmas is . . . Heather
sitting in the bathtub,
washing hair ribbons
and listening to Dylan
Thomas's "A Child's
Christmas in Wales" over
public radio.*

EASY HOLIDAYS

SEVENTEEN

Have Yourself a Very Merry . . .

I bring you good tidings of great joy . . . (Luke 2:10, KJV).

I'm not sure what Christmas says about me and my family, though I'm sure it says something. For Christmas, more than any other season of the year, is a time when our values are expressed at a maximum level.

I remember my childhood Christmases as being filled to the brim with wonder, joy, love, and even a sense of unity with mankind. As an adult, however, I often find myself approaching this holiday with feelings of anxiety. I am frustrated with high prices, busy with demanding schedules, and worried that I might not quite live up to my responsibilities as a parent during this special time. And no matter how hard I try, I am never able to recreate those wonderful Christmases of days past.

How did Mother stretch the dollar to make our gift stacks so enormously high? What did she do to give the house that sweet, pungent aroma of its own? And how did she ever make all of the days leading up to Christmas morning so rich and meaningful to us?

Perhaps by the time Heather is grown, I shall have found the answers. Meanwhile, I am learning to be content with the knowledge that I don't have to recreate the celebrations of my childhood. All I have to do as a Christian mother is help my

family remember whose birthday we are celebrating. This
I do with a sense of freedom that only the gift of God's Son
can bring.

■ We practice a modified form of Christmas simplicity
at our house. Only the dining room is decorated. This not
only cuts down on expenditures, but enables Heather to
feast her eyes upon the Christmas tree during dinner—an
important consideration to those of us who spend the day
away from home!

■ We open the holiday season with the ritual of addressing
Christmas cards—an expense that I generously allow
for in our Christmas budget. In today's impersonal world,
I place a high value on sending Christmas greetings
through the mail to our friends.

■ We help Heather save money for a children's shoe fund,
collected during our church's Christmas Eve service. It is
so easy to get caught up in our own family's Christmas
that doing for others often calls for real planning and
foresight.

■ We begin Christmas morning with a British-style tea, with
lots of sandwiches, jellies, sweets, biscuits, and a thickly
whipped eggnog. To accommodate this feast, I bake weeks
ahead of time, storing my goodies in the freezer. I also
feel free to purchase what I need from the bakery. (As long
as it's good, no one really cares whose oven it came from.)

■ We give homemade, secondhand, or inexpensive appropriate gifts. A few examples from my idea list follow.

For the reader: A very back issue of a magazine. Magazines
reached the height of their glory during the fifties—you'll
find that back issues from this era still provide excellent
reading.

For the cook: A recipe collection—either your own, or a
cut-and-paste version of your magazine favorites.

For grandparents: A scrapbook of your children's schoolwork.

For relatives: A picture frame for their child. The trick is that you take a candid shot ahead of time and slip it into the frame before you give it away.

For the teenage girl: Belts, costume jewelry, and scarves from a secondhand store.

For the writer: A decorative pencil sharpener, a box of pencils from the office supply store, and a yellow legal pad.

For a spouse: Something he or she would have to purchase eventually, accompanied by a handwritten limerick or love poem.

For the boss: A box full of gag gifts—each representing some aspect of your daily work. (Most of these items would be found around the house.)

Feeling comfortable with the idea of inexpensive gift giving and the relaxation of time-worn holiday traditions calls for a change in the way we feel and think about Christmas. But I dare you to give it a try. Somehow, when we accept the freedom of God's love and begin to practice our holiday options, we know for sure that the star in Bethlehem is still shining—even today.

There are, of course, times when an alternative or simplified Christmas just isn't appropriate for a family's situation. For instance, one Christian woman related the brokenness of not having had Christmas as a child.

"Once we had gifts," she said, "but they were not wrapped. There was never a tree, no special cooking, and certainly no singing."

Today, this woman perceives the creation of a special Christmas celebration as part of her family ministry. Serving her loved ones in this way has helped heal the scars of an unhappy childhood.

And there are other reasons for pulling out the stops at Christmas. Perhaps there's been an economic or emotional crisis during the year, and Mom senses the need for some extra special celebrating. A serious illness, death, or birth are additional reasons families give for planning an unusually elaborate Christmas. And many families tell of having some very special Christmases intermingled with quite sparse and simple ones.

This is all to say that Christmas doesn't have to be celebrated in any particular form or fashion. The important thing to remember is that we are celebrating the gift of God's Son. Secure in his infinite love, we can use this season as a time of developing the uniqueness of family tradition . . . however elaborate or simple that may be.

Families build holiday traditions in a variety of ways. Some customs are brought to a marriage from each partner's childhood. Others spontaneously arise within the family as it grows, while still others are borrowed from outside sources such as friends and reading resources. Though it's true some families are stronger on tradition than others, almost every family has at least one original Christmas idea or custom. Begin asking people how they celebrate the holiday . . . being careful to listen for details. You'll soon have a collection of wonderful activities to add to your family's fun. Here are some ideas to get you started.

TWENTY-ONE CHRISTMAS IDEAS
FROM CHRISTIAN WORKING MOTHERS

1. Keep on track by reading the Christmas story several times throughout the holiday season. Use different Bible versions and uncover new thoughts.

2. Plan a thematic Christmas. Select a central theme; coordinate decorations, cooking, and family activities around this theme. One woman who follows such a plan begins thinking about her theme in August so that there's plenty of time for simple sewing projects or the collection of ideas. Some examples: star Christmas, angel Christmas, teddy-bear Christmas, Christmas around the world, an old-fashioned Christmas, and a "Happy Birthday, Jesus" Christmas.

3. Make "Good News" sacks. Type Scripture verses on narrow strips of paper. Fold and stuff into little drawstring cloth bags. Hang these on the tree to give as

favors to people who come through your home during
the holidays. (If there's absolutely no time to make the
bags, you can gain the same effect by using the tiny
paper favor sacks sold at card shops.)

4. Dress children in colorful clothing when Christmas
shopping—they'll be easier to keep an eye on in large
crowds.

5. Set up a card table of gift wrap materials in some
remote corner of your house . . . so the mess is contained in one small area.

6. Participate as a family in a community project. Coins
saved from lunch money, etc., may be used to help feed
the hungry or support a mission concern in your church.
A nearby natural disaster might give your family a
chance to become more personally involved in helping
others.

7. For interesting entertainment at large family gatherings,
appoint an older child to sneak around and record
conversations while guests are gathering. Play the tape
back during dessert or after gifts have been opened.

8. Hang ribbons of different lengths from the top of a door
frame. Tie a Christmas ball at each end.

9. Pin Christmas balls to your drapes.

10. Use baskets for displaying small gifts or holiday arrangements of greenery and pine cones.

11. Turn an ordinary casserole into a festive dish by decorating with a wreath of parsley.

12. Allow the children to decorate plain paper plates and
napkins with stickers or construction paper cutouts. Use
these for holiday breakfasts and lunches. A variation:
Trim plain plastic glasses, placemats, coffee cups, and
plates with strips of red and green tape.

13. Make a "program" for visiting relatives. Include a
schedule of activities such as a midnight church service,
gift exchange, and Christmas day hike. The Christmas
dinner menu and a meaningful Christmas poem can
also be added. Make copies on a copy machine and
paste onto special paper (purchased at a print shop).
Bind with gold braid.

14. Cover the inside of your front door with red felt held in place with double-faced tape. It makes an ideal spot for displaying Christmas cards.

15. Create a Christmas atmosphere by using lots of candles, evergreen boughs (found at local tree lots), and Christmas music. Simmer cinnamon sticks on the stove for a delicious, spicy aroma.

16. Attend a church Christmas program as a family. Stop for hot chocolate on the way home.

17. Have a white Christmas no matter where you live. Wrap all gifts in white; plan decorations of white on white; and teach the children to sing "White Christmas."

18. For an inexpensive decoration, group Christmas tree balls of different sizes amid greenery on a tray.

19. Whenever you're not using serving pieces, make them a festive part of your holiday decor. Fill them with tinsel, greens, or glass ornaments. This saves you from putting such pieces back on those high shelves where they usually reside . . . and keeps them readily available for the next party.

20. Adopt a Christmas mystery friend. Send him/her periodic gifts and cards throughout the season. If you do this within an organization, you can have a final party at which Christmas friends are identified.

21. Display a jar of red hots (candy) on the living room mantel, not to be opened until the Christmas tree is taken down.

Working mothers are unanimous that pulling off a memorable Christmas takes careful planning and organization. One way to effectively meet your holiday needs is to build a working Christmas calendar *before* the month of December. Here is an example of what your calendar might look like.

DECEMBER

1. Make Christmas plans.
   a. Where will you spend Christmas?
   b. With whom?

    c. Which meals will you be responsible for?

    d. What parties will you attend?

2. Purchase Christmas idea magazines. Check out Christmas books from the library.

3. Select and purchase Christmas cards.

4. Make lists.

    a. Gift lists.

    b. Christmas card lists. (Appoint older children to begin addressing envelopes.)

    c. Party guests list.

    d. Gift wrapping needs list.

    e. Grocery and household supplies list.

5. Meditate on the Christmas story.

6. Post a calendar of family activities. Contact a babysitter in advance for adult parties.

7. Begin making homemade tree decorations.

8. Decide on a new tradition.

9. Decorate the tree. Serve popcorn and Cokes for refreshment.

10. Take a day off work and go Christmas shopping. Hints to make it easier:

    a. Shop by phone.

    b. Shop in the morning.

    c. Finish gift list before going.

    d. Use shops that don't draw Christmas crowds—hardware shops, art supply stores, antique stores, etc.

11. Mail Christmas cards and packages.

12. Plan Christmas dinner menu.

13. Clean out closets; organize clothing; make certain party clothes are in good condition. Help children make room for new toys to come.

14. Rest.

15. Have an old-fashioned candy-making night.

16. Take the children shopping—treat them to a cup of eggnog once home.

17. Gift wrap night.

18. Family game night.

19. Rest. Read Christmas stories and poetry aloud.

20. Make certain tablecloth, napkins, and silver are clean and ready for Christmas dinner.

21. Roast marshmallows and pop popcorn over fireplace fire.
22. Drive through town viewing special lights.
23. Take gifts of fruit or homemade goodies to friends.
24. Family Christmas Eve party—exchange names and allow each person to open the name-draw gift.
25. Christmas Day—open gifts, serve coffee cake, attend church, and eat a scrumptious dinner.

Now build your own calendar!

GIFT WRAP IDEAS

One of the best ways to dazzle your friends and family with a Christmas gift is to wrap it beautifully and imaginatively. Working mothers may be inclined to shop at stores that offer gift wrapping services, but a commercially wrapped gift rarely looks like anything else. On the other hand, by taking a few moments to plan ahead, you can create special, individualized gift wraps for the people you love.

The first step in creative wrapping is to set up a card table in some untrafficked area of your house. Stock it with all the trimmings you'll need for decorating packages. Then wrap at your own pace and convenience.

Select gifts that come in attractive packages, and you'll have a head start. Often, you'll find the outer container of your gift needs only a ribbon or a bow to complete its festive look.

Sewing or notions departments yield a variety of imaginative trimmings. Lace, buttons, yarn, and fabric are just a few of the items that can turn a humble gift into a treasured Christmas decoration.

Those who can't sew can always glue. With a glue stick, write a message across the top of your wrapped gift; then sprinkle with glitter for a stunning effect.

Looking for an unusual wrapping medium? Try wrapping your gift in felt, flocked acrylic wallpaper, newsprint, aluminum foil, or a road map. Never settle for the predictable bow. Tie your gift with rickrack, hair ribbon, or a clothing trim such as a belt or men's tie. You may also add interest by decorating with a snapshot, pretty seals, tiny pine cones, holly, mistletoe, or sea shells.

And if you really want to make a hit with the recipient, top your gift with an extra gift: a roll of film, sachet, special soap, a box of crayons, and so on.

You'll find these added touches will make gift wrapping more fun. Besides, your gifts will be just as appreciated beneath the tree as when they are finally opened.

Then they opened their presents and gave him gold, frankincense and myrrh (Matthew 2:11b, TLB).

FOR RECORDING RECEIVED CHRISTMAS CARDS . . .
THIS YEAR 19____
WE RECEIVED SEASON'S GREETINGS
FROM . . .

_____

_____

_____

_____

_____

_____

_____

_____

_____

_____

_____

_____

_____

_____

_____

_____

_____

_____

_____

_____

_____

_____

_____

_____

TO HELP CHILDREN WITH THANK-YOU LETTERS . . .
WE MUST WRITE THESE
"THANK YOU" LETTERS

To _____
For _____
From _____

To _____
For _____
From _____

To _____
For _____
From _____

To _____
For _____
From _____

To _____
For _____
From _____

To _____
For _____
From _____

TAKING THE SPIRIT OF CHRISTMAS TO WORK

Many of these ideas would require permission from the
appropriate department.

1. Hang a small wreath on your office door or outer cubicle
   wall.
2. Organize a lunch hour cookie exchange.
3. Collect Christmas recipes from employees; type up
   and run off on the copy machine and staple into booklets
   to be distributed to all employees.
4. Hold a coloring contest for the children of employees.
   Hang finished art in the company's lunchroom. Reward
   each participant with a small token such as candy.

5. Invite employees to participate in a paper snowflake contest. Hang each intricately cut snowflake in the lunchroom or hallway. Reward the winner with a snowflake tree ornament.
6. Set up a Christmas puzzle table in the lunchroom for employees to work on during break and lunch hour.
7. Purchase a Christmas brooch or earrings to wear throughout the holiday season.

OTHER HOLIDAYS TO CELEBRATE

NEW YEAR'S DAY
Invite another family or two to share in your holiday party.
Serve: Sloppy Joes, chips, dips, beans, fresh salad, black-eyed peas for "good luck," brownies, coffee, and Cokes.
Tell children to bring one favorite toy, and ask women who don't like football to bring needlework.
Give inexpensive date books as favors.

VALENTINE'S DAY
Make homemade valentines for family members. Several days before the date, set up a table with lace, paper, ribbons, seals, stickers, etc. Allow family members to select supplies before going off to a private spot to compose their creations.

Write a love poem to your husband.

Search your Bible for messages about the heart.
Psalm 139:23, 24
Proverbs 4:23
Proverbs 23:7a
Matthew 5:8
Matthew 15:19
Luke 12:34
John 14:1
Romans 10:10

EASTER
Before Easter:
1. Purchase new clothes for the children or spiff up old garments with new trims. Talk about how new clothing

symbolizes a new beginning through Christ.
2. Bake or purchase special bread for Easter breakfast.
3. On Good Friday try a modified fast. No breakfast and only soup for lunch.

Easter morning:
1. Present each child with an Easter basket of real Easter eggs, trinkets, a few pieces of candy, and a Bible bookmark with "Christ Is Risen" written on it.
2. Attend church.
3. Lunch out at a good restaurant or serve a special meal at home using your best china and silver. (Invite another Christian family to join you.)
4. Have an indoor or backyard egg hunt. Make a map for your hunt; tape it inside an empty egg carton in which the hunter can store the chocolate or hard-boiled treasures.

JULY 4TH
1. Fly a flag above your front door.
2. Attend a local parade.
3. Make homemade ice cream.
4. Eat hot dogs for lunch.
5. Go swimming as a family.
6. Watch fireworks.
7. Thank God for our freedom.

THANKSGIVING
1. Thanksgiving away from home? Share your meal with another family and ward off homesickness with the blending of traditions.
2. Have a cranberry guessing contest. Fill a dish with fresh cranberries. Each guest ventures a guess as to the number of cranberries in the dish. The berries are counted and presented as a gift to the person making the closest guess.
3. Prepare a turkey table. Equip a card table with raw potatoes, construction paper, toothpicks, and other imaginative turkey-making gear. Let children make turkeys while parents watch the televised football game.
4. Offer a Thanksgiving box. Decorate a shoe box; place a

stack of notecards and pencils beside it. Invite everyone to write what they're thankful for on a piece of paper and insert into box. Read the anonymous notes during dessert.
5. Dress up your Thanksgiving table. Halve a scooped-out pineapple. The leaves become a turkey's tail feathers. Make a head and neck out of construction paper or poster board. Fasten with toothpicks. Fill with fruit salad. Twist sprigs of grapevine to make unique napkin rings.

STILL MORE HOLIDAYS TO CELEBRATE

Celebrations don't have to be major holidays. Break the monotony of everyday life by celebrating the little things.

1. On George Washington's birthday, stop by the store on your way home and pick up a cherry pie. A simple statement such as, "Today was George Washington's birthday and we're having a cherry pie because he cut down a cherry tree when he was a little boy" will make the meal a festive occasion.
2. On each family member's birthday, allow the birthday person to decide where and what he'd like to eat that night.
3. Celebrate good report cards with ice cream sundaes.
4. Remember to wear green on St. Patrick's Day—even if you're not Irish.
5. Plant a tree in your yard on Arbor Day. *Give* a tree to a new home owner if your yard has its quota.

Most important, don't let working be an excuse for not celebrating life. Live each day to its fullest. Have fun at work —then relax at home and continue having fun. Sure, you may be tired. But settle for feeling less than great every now and then to enrich your family's life with memories of happy times.

FROM MY JOURNAL
*Barbra writes me that
_____ is being
divorced by her husband.
I feel threatened and
pained and then sur-
prised at my vivid
emotions. I thought I
had divorce all figured
out! Now, the reality of
sweet, kind, loving
_____ not being
loved in return makes me
feel vulnerable all over
again.*

*What upsets me the
most, however, is that
there isn't the strong
endorsement of marriage
from society at large
that there used to be.
Not even the church is as
opposed to divorce as it
once was. So, if success-
ful marriage is next to
impossible, why did
Jesus give us such exact
commands concerning
it? I wonder if he would
be more flexible
today . . . or if the same
rules still apply?*

*And when people ask,
I am reserved about my
own happy marriage;
matrimony doesn't come
with a written guaran-
tee.*

ENJOYING MARRIAGE

EIGHTEEN

Happily Ever After

During medical school, student marriages followed the law of the jungle—only the fittest survived. Every fall, the auxiliary newsletter contained a small box with this ominous notice: "Due to unusual circumstances, the following offices need to be refilled." The reality of possible divorce in our lives was accepted early on; some couples would make it all the way through school—others would not. So, we learned to become sophisticated in our outlook toward marriage and not to show surprise at the latest divorce news. After all, not everyone wants to be married to a doctor, anyway. But for those of us who did want to be married and stay married to our particular doctor, the challenge was almost overwhelming.

Today, I don't think any of us survivors would stand up and smugly give advice on how to stay happily married. We still live in such fragile glass houses ourselves. And yet, because a woman's personal growth inevitably has some effect upon her marriage, I felt it important to address this subject by highlighting the knowns in my own marriage. Obviously, I can't make guarantees on my marriage or yours. But what I can do is share a few of the things that have worked for Olie and me and some of the things that have not.

WHAT WORKS FOR US

I believe there are basically two factors necessary for a successful marriage. First, we have to acknowledge that marriage is the union of two independent beings who bring their individuality to the altar as a means of enriching the union. Though you've heard it a thousand times before, I would caution you against trying to remake your spouse or yourself. To blend into one is to become a stalemate and invites the very dangerous ingredient of boredom into your lives. Second, it's important to realize that a marriage has to be developed— not just in the early years, but for its duration. We can never afford the luxury of not working at our marriage. People usually accept both of these facts readily enough, but, unfortunately, do very little about them.

So that you don't have to fall into the latter group, here are a few hints to aid you in the nourishment of your marriage.

1. Do the unpredictable now and then . . . the things you may want to do but that don't fit in with other people's perception of you. Dance the flame dance after dinner, serve a cheese tray instead of a meal, take flying lessons, wear outrageous costume jewelry. . . .

   As Olie and I journeyed out of our twenties, we noticed a curious thing. Our marriage was revitalized as each of us rediscovered our old selves. Talents and hobbies that had been shelved for years suddenly reappeared and we were more like the Olie and Jayne of our dating years than the Olie and Jayne of early marriage.

   In a recent newspaper article, clinical social worker Gay Jurgens gave boredom as a major cause of divorce. She said that in the case of a dual-career marriage, home often becomes little more than a resting place. When a couple's entire energy is turned to separate careers, there's simply none left for the development of the marriage.

   So really work on being an interesting person full of surprises. Keep the brain stimulated with learning, accept life's challenges, and experiment with the "new." Forget about your job and take a camping trip or join forces with your husband on a community project. You'll be surprised at how even small things can give you more to talk about and make you feel closer.

2. Be responsible for your own state of happiness, then share it joyously with your spouse. Keep in mind that it isn't your spouse's responsibility to make you happy. Get out and find friends, hobbies, or a job that will make you happy.

During especially low points in our lives, Olie and I have a tendency to lean heavily on each other for personal happiness. It almost never works. It usually isn't until we seek out those things that make us whole as individuals that life begins to fall into place.

3. Tune in to your spouse's concerns. True soul mates share each other's goals and aspirations. Some of these goals deserve joint efforts, while others need only your sincere and enthusiastic interest.

Getting through medical school was a joint project for Olie and me. But Olie's listening to my continuous mono-logue on writing projects was vital proof of his interest in me and was just as important as my helping to pay the bills.

Periodically, working couples need to examine their life together to ask themselves if they're truly satisfied with their present life. Dissatisfaction can then be worked out by compromising or making a total life-style change.

Invariably, success comes for one partner while the other is still "waiting." It's not easy to rejoice and be happy for your spouse in such instances—but it's abso-lutely imperative that you try! Celebrate each victory with dinner out, a cake from the bakery, or a congratulatory note. Attend each other's company parties. Make an effort to memorize names and faces of your spouse's fellow employees. Be willing to promote his work with any special skills you may have, or by entertaining the boss. Ask questions about his work. Learn to share the exciting and meaningful aspects of yours—don't just bring home the problems. When couples are genuinely interested in each other's careers, loss of interest in the marriage is less likely to happen.

The road may be more difficult if you're married to

a super-achiever, however. Mary Alice Kellogg, author of *Fast Track: The Super Achievers,* says such people are often self-centered and it's important to realize *you* won't get the nurturing you may desire from such a mate. The super-achiever is rarely home.

And *his* job always comes first. It can be very discouraging to have to pack up and leave your good job to follow this man around the country. But if this is your problem, be patient and wait upon the Lord. Let your career take a back seat for now. A part-time job in your field or the pursuit of an advanced degree will keep your knowledge and skills updated. In the meantime, do have a life of your own. Those married to super-achievers need to develop a strong self-identity and be able to enjoy living—even in their husband's absence.

4. Treat your spouse with the same tenderness you showed during courtship. Here are some specific ideas:
    a. Listen to him carefully.
    b. Say thank you.
    c. Make something special for him—a sweater, a cake, etc.
    d. Send him flowers.
    e. Touch him often, but never hang on him.
    f. Play a special song on the jukebox for him.
    g. Put a favorite candy bar in his briefcase.
    h. When sending him off on a business trip, pack your picture and one of the children in the middle of his suitcase.
    i. Mail a card to his office.
    j. Greet him at the end of the day with a hug.

SPECIAL POINTERS

■ Always resolve your differences before retiring for the night. Sometimes after an argument, people do wake up determined to put yesterday behind them. But it's probably more common for unresolved arguments to quietly smolder until the next big flareup.

- Make appointments with each other. A "date" per week is not a luxury, but an essential element for a healthy, happy marriage. If finances are tight and the cost of a baby-sitter is prohibitive, talk with other Christian mothers about forming a Friday night baby-sitting co-op.
- Don't spend all your weekend time catching up on chores. Take Saturday or Sunday afternoon off to go to the lake or country. When you must tackle housecleaning, be clear about the division of chores with a written contract.
- Rather than waste time arguing or pouting, decide together what kind of activities you will or will not participate in on your time off. The same can be said about which people you will or won't spend time with. Be careful not to schedule every minute—allow for free time so you won't always be in a hurry.
- Telephone each other for a brief chat during the work day. Jog together in the evening. Stay up late one night a week.
- Things that don't work for us:
  1. Discussing faults.
  2. Keeping secrets.
  3. Interrupting.

CONDITIONS TO BE AVOIDED

Certain conditions really do seem harmful to sound marriages, but you can control many of these factors so that your marriage environment is a healthy one.

Unhealthy conditions that you can control are:

- Lack of privacy—when children are allowed to stay up too late in the evenings.
- Noise pollution—there is always background noise coming from either the television or radio.
- Poor self-image—one or both spouses suffer from lack of self-respect.

Most of all, it's important to remember that people who have good marriages aren't any smarter, better, or luckier than those who don't. The difference is primarily in the fact that these people simply believe in marriage. Those of us who have been married long enough to beat the national odds may give the impression of leading perfect lives and having it all together—but we don't. We, too, have problems with money, boredom, jealousy, and the like. But we believe in marriage to the extent that we work these problems out within the marriage. In this respect, I hope all of us who are happily married will lend support to other married couples. People need to be reassured that in spite of the world's message, divorce isn't the only way to improve one's situation.

With a lot of work and perseverance, we can find ourselves, enjoy happiness, and know true freedom, all within the bounds of matrimony.

"Therefore what God has joined together, let man not separate" (Matthew 19:6, NIV).

FROM MY JOURNAL
*Last night five-year-old
Heather came to me
with a prayer request.*

*"Mommy," she said,
"when you pray tonight
will you do me a favor?
Will you ask God to
change the whole
world?"*

*"Why, Heather,
whatever do you mean
by that?" I asked.*

*"I just want our life to
be beautiful," she
answered. "I want a
pretty house instead of
this one. I want a flower
garden instead of our
ugly yard. I want. . . ."*

*Heather's wishes
trailed on as I stood
there staring helplessly
into her questioning
eyes. The time had come
for me to say the right
thing—something about
values, priorities, and
Christ's desire for our
lives. But I was tired,
and when my mouth
opened, out came a
snarling, curt reprimand.*

*"Don't be silly," I said.
"You know as soon as
your father gets out of
school we're going to live
in a decent neighbor-
hood. We do the best we
can. Now get to sleep."*

HOME DECORATING:

NINETEEN

They Say Beauty Isn't Skin Deep

I suppose the most shocking thing about Heather's asking for
a more beautiful life was my failure to have given her one.
Certainly I had worked hard enough on teaching the merits
of a beautiful heart. And naturally I had stressed the importance of caring for one's outer appearance. It was just that
somewhere between putting bread on the table and a husband through medical school, I had completely overlooked
the significance of beautiful surroundings.

What I realize now, however, is that beauty is not something
to be carelessly ignored. It is an essential ingredient of wholesome living—part of God's plan for our lives. And surpris-
ingly enough, it is accessible to all, regardless of our economic
status. True, inspiring, uplifting beauty isn't, as so many of us
have come to believe, the display of valuable possessions.
True beauty is the kind we see in God's creation; beauty that
works for the good of mankind.

We don't have to go into debt to bring this kind of beauty
into our lives. All we need is a sense of duty and a willingness
to accept the creativity of the Holy Spirit. But how can these
qualities make for a cozy home?

Lord, you have been our dwelling place throughout all generations (Psalm 90:1, NIV).

There are several ways to find the right house for your family. Check the real estate section of your local newspaper for an outstanding "desperation" sale. Spend weekends driving through neighborhoods you'd like to live in. You'll find models and open houses for your inspection. Enlist the aid of a real estate broker whose representative will do most of the actual footwork for you. But whatever method of hunting you choose, don't try to store all of your impressions in your memory. Keep a list of all houses visited, being sure to record the address, price, owner's name, and all features present or missing. You may even want to take a photograph of the exterior of the house.

Don't be surprised if the process of choosing a new home begins to feel like work. It is! Making the transaction seem of even greater magnitude is the semi-permanent nature of the purchase. There's no provision for exchange or refunds here. But handled with prudence, your home-buying venture can be a pleasant one, bringing you many years of satisfaction. To make this happen, however, consider several factors.

ADVICE FOR THE HOME BUYER

Realtors say the single most important factor to consider when buying a house is location. Of course, a good location means different things to different people. For one person it may mean living close to work. For others, it may imply a wholesome family environment with a prestigious school system. And for still others, a good location has more to do with the feeling and atmosphere of "establishment" rather than convenience.

Another very important factor for house-hunters to consider is financing. Here's where a professional realtor can help by introducing you to creative financing alternatives. He knows which lenders are making current loans, at what rate, and for what amount. Realtors also help people determine what price range they need to consider when selecting a new home. If a realtor knows what you can afford, he'll find you a house in that price range. And sometimes there are great variances, depending upon whether or not the home is owner-financed or a nonescalating assumable loan. At any rate, a realtor knows the market and can save you the headaches and time of probing.

Then, too, there is the question of quality. Whether you're considering a new house or an older one, quality construction is crucial. How does one determine the quality of the "unseeables"—hidden factors in construction and lot value?

To be truthful, you'll have to rely mostly upon the integrity of the builder, owner, or real estate agent. But here are a few questions you can ask that should point you toward a good buy.

1. Is the house built on fill land? If so, it may be on unsteady footing and could shift unduly.
2. Are the windows insulated or double glazed? If not, they aren't energy efficient.
3. Does the house have termite protection? Ask for written evidence from a pest-control company.
4. How effective is the wall insulation?
5. Is the floor beneath the carpet finished? If not, and you decide against wall-to-wall carpeting, you'll have to finish it yourself.
6. Does the house have adequate electrical service? The entrance should range from 100 to 200 amp.
7. Is the plumbing system hooked into the city sewer? If the system is on a septic tank, make sure it has the capacity to handle your needs.
8. Is the inside diameter of the plumbing pipes at least 1/2 inch? On a good plumbing job, 3/4-inch pipe is used for all main runs.
9. Are the heating and cooling systems on separate circuits? If not, you could have a shortage of electrical power. All large appliances should also be on separate circuits.

If you have a family member or friend who is in construction, you may want to ask him to look over your choice. His trained eye can quickly spot things you might miss on your own.

Once you are satisfied that the construction of the house is solid, take another look indoors. Now is the time to reconsider your own personal needs in a home. These too are important and should not be hastily sacrificed. Your checklist of desirable features might look something like this:

1. Are the windows positioned to make use of sunlight and a pleasant view?
2. Is the floor plan such that some degree of privacy can be granted to each family member?
3. Is there adequate kitchen cabinet and counter-top space?
4. Is the existing floorcovering appropriate to the family's life-style and decorating scheme?
5. Are the closets large enough?
6. Are the bathrooms easily accessible to all bedrooms?
7. Are the washer/dryer connections in an acceptable area?
8. Are the electrical outlets at convenient sites?
9. Is the air flow such that the house receives good ventilation when the windows are open?
10. Are the rooms large enough to hold existing furniture? (Measure with a tape measure.)

Finally, take one last walk through and visualize your furnishings in place. Then imagine your family at home in this house. If they seem to fit—chances are your house-hunting days are over.

But what if you can't afford the type of house you really want, or find that you have to settle for the temporary arrangement of renting a house or an apartment? In such a case, it may help to reconsider what a home really is.

Think on the qualities that mean home—comfort, love, care, order, beauty. All of these traits can be brought into our homes without economic prosperity; they are always affordable. We can always make certain that the furnishings in our home are comfortable, that the atmosphere is one of Christian love, that the interior and exterior are clean and well cared for, that possessions are arranged in an orderly manner, and that some type of beauty (howbeit simple) is employed to lift spirits. And when these are the qualities we're striving for, preconceived notions about decorating, neighborhoods, and

even architectural styles will give way to freer forms of
expression.

DECORATING WITH COLOR

Now that you've found your home, what about the interior
environment? One of the most important and easy-to-use
tools is color. Anyone who has ever been refreshed by the cool
hues of plant life or calmed by the serenity of a sunset can
appreciate the influence of color upon our lives.

. . . He maketh me to lie down in green pastures . . .
(Psalm 23:2, KJV).

Though not always inexpensive, a bucket of paint can
do more toward creating room personality and making a
statement about you, the homemaker, than anything else. If
you don't own a house, you may be reluctant to paint because
of rent deposit rules or the impracticality of spending money
on a temporary dwelling. My advice is to forget the deposit.
And would painting your own home be any more permanent?
Probably not, when we stop to consider that handprints and
other day-to-day grime make painting a periodic necessity.
Here are interesting ways to decorate with paint.

1. Enhance a young girl's room by painting the woodwork a
   different value or intensity of the wall paint. Example:
   pink walls and raspberry woodwork.
2. Add interest to a wall by rag-rolling, a technique which
   produces textured surfaces by applying a strip of paint in
   the highlight color on top of the dry base color and then
   rolling over it with a twisted, lint-free cloth while it is still
   wet.
3. Transform an ordinary child's room with a mural depicting a scene from a familiar children's book. You can
   give the illusion of space by painting a pretend window
   complete with the view of outdoor scenery on a window-
   less wall. (No artistic ability? Commission an art student
   to help out.)
4. Personalize a room with hand-painted furniture. Stencils

will help you make appealing borders and sophisticated designs.

5. Create bold drama by painting one wall of a room a darker shade of the predominant color. Example: Paint three walls kelly green; paint the far wall a darker forest green.

Of course, painting isn't the only means of utilizing color. Draperies, furniture, and accessories can all update and refresh the home by color choice alone.

When thinking about colors, it's often helpful to consider a color wheel (found in paint or art stores). You'll notice one half of the wheel is made up of cool colors, the other warm. The warm colors are called the sun colors: red, yellow, and orange. The cool colors are the evening colors: blue, green, and purple.

Because colors are an illusionary medium, there's an art to selecting tones and combinations. For instance, colors appear brighter when used in large areas. So when choosing wall color, select a less intense shade than you think you want. You can make a large room feel smaller and cozier or make a high ceiling appear lower by using bold, bright colors. Pastels, on the other hand, will make a small room seem more spacious.

A color is always affected by the color next to it—appearing lighter when placed next to a dark color, and darker when near a light hue. Creating a color scheme is really nothing more than choosing one main hue, and highlighting it with a variety of toner hues.

If you're satisfied with a particular color scheme in your home, check the color patterns with a color wheel. You'll probably find you have instinctively chosen one of the color schemes given below. Much of our color knowledge came to us as children when our own mothers surrounded us with pleasing combinations . . . more evidence of the importance of our developing the art ourselves.

COMMON COLOR SCHEMES
Monochromatic—using one color in many values and intensities.

A single woman I know has used this scheme in pink. Her sofa is upholstered in a nubby tea rose print fabric. The walls are a delicate hint of pink, the drapes a soft feminine flux of rose-colored sheers, and the carpet a hardy, soil-resistant mauve shade. Pillows and other accessories are all pleasing tones, tints, and shades of the one single color, and the result is absolutely delightful.

Related or analogous—combining hues which are side by side on the color wheel and which have the same color base. Usually up to five colors can be successfully used.

Try related colors for a cheerful, country look. You might select a sandy, soft beige and rose chintz print sofa, arm chairs upholstered in rose stripes, pale yellow print valances to let in plenty of sunlight, and yellow checked throw pillows for accent.

Triadic—a harmony that combines three colors equidistant on the color wheel.

A woman who lives in a very small condominium made her tiny living area seem larger by selecting peach as the predominant decorating color. Peach carpeting, a textured sofa of peach print, and a forest green accent chair helped convey the feeling of spaciousness. The woman then picked up the forest green in a cornice board above white mini-blinds and threw deep purple pillows on the sofa for a truly impressive upscale look.

Complementary—using opposite colors on the color wheel.

An eye-pleasing example of this scheme is the blue and orange combination. For a refreshing, contemporary look, you might choose a blue velour sofa, arm chairs upholstered in orange print, blue Roman shades, and orange throw pillows. Any accessories would feature shades of orange or blue, or perhaps pick up a pale green from blue's analogous neighbor.

Split complementary—one color combined with the two colors adjacent to its complement.

A bright, sunny interpretation of this color scheme would be a floral-patterned sofa of rosy pink and yellow printed on a deep blue violet. Matching drapes along with a matching love seat would then be complemented by a comfortable chair in a coordinating yellow print. Accessories such as pink silk roses on the coffee table would complete this charming atmosphere.

Double split complementary—two pairs of colors adjacent to one pair of complementary colors.

A room decorated in this format is certain to be charged with exciting individuality. Imagine a purple carpet, yellow-orange love seats, and chairs of soft velour with purple throw pillows and splashes of bright red-violet accessories throughout. Definitely not a design for the color-timid person!

Achromatic colors—black, gray, and white are referred to as neutrals or colorless. They may be used with any color harmony.

Don't confine the use of your color wheel to the living room area. You can use the same techniques in your kitchen, bedrooms, and baths. As you plan, respect your own likes and dislikes while paying attention to your family's life-style. If there are small children or rowdy boys at home, you may opt for darker floorcoverings and upholstery. But today's pastel carpets are specially treated to take considerable wear and tear, as are many fabrics; so you may not have to sacrifice as much as you think. And do put out accessories—children and adults both need the lift of interesting or beautiful objects around. Just use them sparingly and wisely. Children don't understand monetary value, and busy mothers really shouldn't burden themselves with too many accessories to dust and care for anyway. Also, remember that if you like to rearrange furniture, don't invest in heavy furniture that's difficult to move by yourself.

INEXPENSIVE DECORATING IDEAS
Pulling your family's hobbies into the home decor will provide inexpensive accessories while identifying each member's interests and personality.

Books—If you're a reading family, you're in luck. Nothing looks more comfortable than a book-lined wall, and the old college stand-by of boards and bricks can still make an attractive bookshelf for your home if you varnish the 2 x 4s to a high shine and select bricks for particular color variations.

Corks and cement blocks can also add interest.

Plants—A lot has been said on the value of decorating with houseplants. Now I'm going to say something absolutely unforgivable to plant lovers. Sometimes our homes just aren't suited to plant life—improper lighting or lack of humidity seems to get them every time. If this is true in your home, use dried or silk plants. Making your own arrangements will not only save money but might become an enjoyable hobby as well.

Another alternative to the standard houseplant is water rooting. Place a plant cutting such as ivy in a glass container of water to which a few drops of food coloring have been added. Several containers of different shapes can make a strikingly handsome arrangement suitable for decorating small areas.

Sewing offers all kinds of inexpensive decorating possibilities, but you can get the most decorating mileage for your time and money by sewing up a mound of pillows. The easiest way to make a pillow is to cut your desired shape from inexpensive fabric, sew up three sides, fill it with polyester filling, and hand-sew the remaining open side. A pillow cover—made in exactly the same manner—should then be used to cover this basic form. Omit inserting a zipper, to save time and money. When laundry day comes, you have only to rip out the hand stitching, wash the cover, and re-sew when dry. You can make your covers from inexpensive remnants or old clothing and can recycle worn covers into toys or quilt fabric.

Cloth napkins are another worthwhile sewing project. Besides saving on our natural resources, the use of cloth napkins encourages elegance in everyday living. I sometimes pack one in my daughter's school lunch. She tells me she spreads it out like a tablecloth and everyone asks to join in her picnic. To make napkins: Turn under edge of square cloth ¼ inch. Press in place. Repeat process. Stitch fold down.

Curtains and draperies are another matter—nothing could be more expensive or more important to your surroundings than proper window coverings.*

*Note: Though mini-blinds may seem a reasonable choice for window dressing, when used in the living room, they do require a cornice board in order to look properly "finished." (A fact that still makes curtains your least expensive choice.)

I've found Cape Cod curtains an acceptable way to get around the issue of living room drapes. They're affordable and add a touch of nostalgic charm. You can save even more money by making simple tailored curtains. A casing and hem are all that's required.

CURTAIN INSTRUCTIONS:

1. Measure windows (length and width) after installing fixtures.
2. Add 6" to length and double the width. Divide the width into two panels.
3. Finish the side hems first. Use a 1" double-fold hem on both side and center hems: Turn 2" to underside and press. Turn under cut edges as far as first fold. Stitch close to second fold. Press.
4. For casing, turn 3" at the top edge of curtain to the underside. Press. Turn under cut edge as far as the first fold. Stitch close to the first fold. Stitch close to the second fold. Press.
5. To hem, turn bottom edge 3" to underside. Press. Turn under cut edge ½". Stitch close to second fold. Press.
6. A valance can be made following these same instructions, with length being arbitrarily determined by the length of the curtains.
7. Hang on an old-fashioned expandable curtain rod, available at discount stores.

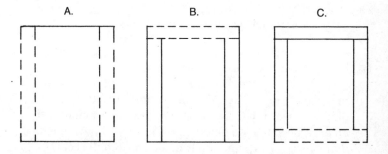

A.   B.   C.

SOMETHING EXTRA . . .
Relax in your own creativity. When it comes to creating a certain look or style, imagination is far more important than

owning particular pieces of furniture. Consider one of these alternatives.

1. You want an Oriental atmosphere but can't afford rattan furniture? Give your Early American furniture the look of faraway places by utilizing the combination of crisp blue and white. Paint your walls sky blue, cover a screen in blue print fabric, and display pieces of blue and white china (which can be inexpensively purchased at import shops).

2. You're fond of the country look but own an assortment of hand-me-downs and do-it-yourself furniture? Give your home rustic unity with lots of natural touches such as baskets, grapevine wreaths, and pillows made from old quilt scraps. Hang dried herbs from the ceiling above the windows, place a table runner down the dining room table, and display plants and candles in lieu of more expensive antique finds. Finally, create an instant, no-fuss slipcover by wrapping the sofa in a colorful quilt.

3. You like everything modern but are stuck with nondescript furniture, upholstered in outdated fabric? Sew or purchase slip covers in solid colors for your upholstered pieces, then simply pare down. Get rid of all but a few really striking accessories. Purchase a brass or chrome reading lamp, hang mini-blinds or sleek shades. The key to your new look is a clean, streamlined environment.

4. Another fun way to add special interest to your home is by placing romantic surprises in various areas.

■ For bedroom romance, you can create an exotic mid-Eastern atmosphere by hanging an Oriental rug (or an inexpensive replica) on the wall behind your bed instead of a headboard. For a more stately aura of romance, utilize an antique gate for a headboard. And for tropical languor, drape a gauzy mosquito netting down from the ceiling over your bed.

■ Soften a too-harsh room by stapling cotton print fabric to the wall.

■ Make a wonderful wall display for your living or dining

- area by mounting old crocheted doilies on fabric and framing.
- Decorate a throw pillow with a lacy, old antimacassar. Simply position on top of a pillow and hand stitch in place.
- Hang lace curtains in your dining area.
- Place a bouquet of silk or fresh flowers in your bathroom.
- Fill a china bowl with rose petals or potpourri and place on your coffee table.

OTHER SUGGESTIONS:

Try aesthetically harmonizing your home with nature. Place the sofa where one can catch an interesting view or perhaps watch the sunset.

Make use of symbolism. Create personal meaning with everyday objects. A lamp table used as a family altar will evoke a special sense of reverence at any time of day.

Keep furnishings and accessories at a minimum. You'll create the illusion of space—a feeling that seems to give rise to deep thoughts and creative actions.

Most important, note that creating beauty in the home is not a problem limited to the financially anemic. I go into houses with the latest of home decor, only to find families hunched over paper plates at the kitchen bar. I visit young mothers whose living room arrangement puts more emphasis on television than conversation. I watch friends quickly shut doors to their children's rooms with the awkward explanation that "they've yet to be decorated." I've had friends whose mothers never "got it together" until we were in college . . . and then it was too late.

Bringing God's beauty into our homes is not an easy matter, and I wouldn't try to make light of it for a moment. Still, I'm willing to give it my best . . . because I'm for homes of Christian heritage. Homes that display the love and beauty of our Lord. Homes that speak of feminine dedication to housekeeping skills. Homes that honor family and friends instead of things. But, of course, before any of this outer tranquility can be achieved in our homes we have to be at peace with God and know that true beauty comes from the Spirit.

. . . the mind controlled by the Spirit is life and peace
(Romans 8:6, NIV).

FROM MY JOURNAL
LEARNING AND BELIEVING*

What I was taught
Never give a child
empty compliments.
Examples:
You're beautiful.
You're special.

What I've learned
People don't grow up knowing
they're beautiful or special unless
someone nurtures them with
supportive statements now and
then. An alternative to empty
compliments might be: "You're
beautiful because God made
you."

*We are the clay; you are the
potter; we are all the work of
your hand* (Isaiah 64:8, NIV).

or

"You're special—God delights
in you."

*He brought me out into a
spacious place; he rescued me
because he delighted in me*
(Psalm 18:19, NIV).

The unknowns
Will helping a child
develop his self-esteem
cause him to become
arrogant or self-
righteous?

Insights
All people need to be told they're
valuable. Not just children, but
husbands and friends, too. God
never stops showing his love for
us. . . .

*"I have loved you with an ever-
lasting love"* (Jeremiah
31:3, NIV).

Nor should we stop openly giving
our love to others.

*ABOUT "LEARNING AND BELIEVING SQUARES"
"Learning and believing squares" are a fun way to explore the issues of your life.
Here's what to do:
   After choosing a subject, divide your paper into four squares. In the first square
write or draw what you've been taught to believe. In the second square express
what you personally have learned through experience. The third square belongs
to the unknown—to all the unresolved knowledge and desires related to the
subject. The fourth square is given to insights and perceptions acquired from
studying the first three squares.

BUILDING SELF-ESTEEM

TWENTY

Learning to Stand Tall

I once overheard a conversation between mother and son.

"Mama," the little boy questioned, "am I handsome?"

I couldn't help but notice he was a very ordinary-looking child with brown hair standing up stubbornly on top of his head and a crop of freckles stretching unmercifully across his nose and cheeks.

"Whatever will she tell him?" I wondered.

Of course, I needn't have worried. The woman answered unfalteringly.

"Yes, dear," she said. "You're the most handsome boy in the world."

Years from now, when that child steps out into the world as a man, I expect to see his shoulders squared and his head held high—for surely such moments build confidence.

Today's Christian parents seem to be on the up and up when it comes to developing our children's self-esteem. We give warm fuzzies and other supportive strokes with fashionable aplomb. But when no one's asking for appraisal, our messages are not always so clear.

I've discovered that on any given day I may unconsciously subject Heather to five or six negative responses in a thirty-minute time span.

"Heather, don't put your feet on the sofa. Goodness, but you're acting like a slob today."

"Heather, what a mess you are. Go put on some decent clothes so we can run our errands."

"Heather, get this trash heap of a room cleaned up, and now."

And I call myself a good parent!

I doubt whether anyone can prove or disprove any long-term effect of "mild" verbal abuse. The point is, such statements are certainly not conveying the message that I as a Christian mother want my speech to give.

I want to respond to my child in a way that will build strong convictions, so she'll have the strength to cope with life's obstacles, the confidence to meet life's changes, the power to master self-control.

This doesn't mean Heather shouldn't be reprimanded for bad habits. It just means that I should take the time to phrase my instructions more pleasantly.

"Heather, don't put your feet on the sofa. We have to take care of our furniture."

"Heather, run and freshen up. People enjoy doing business with clean, well-groomed customers."

"Heather, clean up your room before you got out to play." Isn't that better?

Building self-esteem is not a matter of giving empty compliments. I believe compliments should be given freely and generously, but always with the implication of the inner person's worth.

"You're very pretty," I may say to Heather. "I know you're going to be lovely and kind to your friends today."

And because Heather is blessed with attractiveness and intelligence, I place emphasis on the importance of not criticizing those who are lacking in these areas.

For we are God's workmanship, created in Christ Jesus to do good works, which God prepared in advance for us to do (Ephesians 2:10, NIV). *Your beauty should not come from outward adornment, such as braided hair and the wearing of gold jewelry and fine clothes. Instead, it should be that of your inner self, the unfading beauty of a gentle and quiet spirit, which is of great worth in God's sight* (1 Peter 3:3, 4, NIV).

Each of us has a unique place in God's plan. To reach our potential, we've been given different talents and abilities; our learning takes place at different rates. God never intended for us all to function or look alike—he delights in our specialness. But while we recognize this truth and want our children to have every possible benefit in life, we as busy women sometimes find the business of teaching self-esteem falling by the wayside. Our children may come home from school showing tell-tale signs of inferiority, and we catch ourselves contributing to the problem by saying or doing the wrong thing.

Isn't it a relief, then, to realize that there are so many good things to do in a planned, creative manner which will help develop our little ones' self-esteem? Deciding how we will react to such problems ahead of time will make it easier for us to be the person we'd like to be when a hard day has left us tired and short-tempered. Here are some ideas to try.

THE SMALL CHILD

In the beginning, most of us do everything right. A baby is born and we huddle around him in eager anticipation of each new accomplishment and discovery. We cheer, coax, and encourage so much throughout the day that the baby is certain he really is the hot stuff his family thinks he is. Then, slowly but surely, we begin to take our little miracle for granted. His learning is ordinary—we *expect* him to progress in acceptable fashion. Indeed, anything less would disappoint us. Though he's still quite special in our eyes, we don't feed him the proper nutrients for self-esteem anymore, and when later on he says he never felt as good about himself as the other kids did, we're shocked and a bit hurt.

Thank goodness this degenerative process doesn't have to occur. Today, we know that the art of building positive self-esteem is a continuing process that should be practiced throughout our child's early years and on into adolescence. How to do this is largely up to your own imagination and resourcefulness. But here are some suggestions.

1. Show affection. As your baby grows into childhood and later adolescence, continue to touch, smile, gesture, and speak in a way that shows you care. Verbalize your love for him many times throughout the hours you're together. Children will not just assume we love them—we have to say the words.

2. Give praise freely, making it clear to the young child exactly what it is he has done that's so "right."

3. Don't insist that a child's feelings always be good ones. In her book, *Help Your Child for Life*, Maureen Miller encourages parents to talk about their feelings, illustrating why they may be grouchy, etc. Miller also states that it helps to read your child books dealing with both children's and adults' feelings. Provide plenty of physical outlets for the release of feelings such as climbing gyms, sandboxes, punching bags, and so on.

   Try this simple exercise. Draw four faces on durable posterboard depicting these emotions: happy, sad, angry, OK. Color with markers, cut out, and paste small magnets on the back of each. Place the faces in a shoebox beside the refrigerator. When your child gets up in the morning, he puts it on the refrigerator door. Now you both know how he feels and you can respond to his feelings appropriately.

4. Allow your child to help with housework or some other simple duty. But be realistic in your expectations and always allow for failure.

5. Give your child the opportunity to correct a mistake with dignity. Example: Helping clean up spilled milk. (Praise him for the effort.)

6. Avoid apologizing for a child's unkempt appearance. Children get mussed up at play. If you run into a friend after picking up your child from the baby-sitter or day-care facility, refrain from remarks such as, "Suzie's a little dirty right now—but she usually looks better."

7. Level with your child. It's easier to know where you stand with someone who defines how things will be and why.

8. Provide your child with an area he can call his own—a special place of privacy. If space is at a premium, be creative. When I was a child, I once turned a closet into a

playhouse. Though we must have needed the space, no one ever suggested that I not have this small area of privacy, and it made me feel important.

9. Avoid labeling a child with statements such as "you always . . ." or "you never. . . ."
10. Listen creatively to your child and teach him to do the same. (See chapter 5 for details on this art.)
11. When you must reprimand your child, do it at once, explain how you feel, tell your child you love him, and follow with a hug.
12. Do something special with your child at least once a month. If there is more than one child in your family, allow each to choose one activity a month which he or she can share on a one-to-one basis with you.

THE GROWING CHILD

When your child enters grade school your realm of influence diminishes significantly. Suddenly, people you may not even know are directing the traffic of your child's good and bad feelings. To make things worse, these powerful figures fall somewhere between the ages of six and twelve! All at once, the child you *thought* had a pretty good image of himself is shocking you with open statements of self-doubt. You may find it helpful to impart these simple truths from time to time.

1. Everyone makes mistakes while learning.
2. Not everyone has to like you or what you do; and some people won't!
3. We can expect to be criticized once in awhile because none of us is perfect.
4. Friends move in and out of our lives. Sometimes they leave because they should, and we all survive the unhappy feelings the separation may cause.

As children grow it's still important to make our love known verbally and to cheer, coax, and encourage as much as possible. The elementary years are also a vital time to develop special talents and abilities. People who work with teenage drug rehabilitation programs tell us such abilities help provide a sense of identity and self-worth that may protect our children against the temptation of drug experimentation. But beyond the development of special abilities, this is the time when our children should be exposed to as many different activities as possible. We need to help them understand that perfection is not the point—but that learning many different skills such as swimming and bicycling will make life more enjoyable.

By now, your child will have discovered that some things come easily, while others are more difficult for him. He needs to be encouraged and rewarded for each small improvement in difficult areas. Excellence is growing and grasping toward a goal—not just reaching it.

Finally, your child's physical appearance during elementary years is more important than you may realize. No longer the cute baby, he may need your help in looking his best. Particularly when a child is old enough to select his own clothing, it's easy for busy mothers to overlook haircuts, outgrown clothes, and dirty socks. But children often find themselves ostracized for these oversights. Help your child avoid uncomfortable feelings by taking the time to really look at him before you leave each morning. Spend a weekend revamping his wardrobe if necessary, and indulge his craving for a "popular" clothing item every now and then.

THE TEENAGER

Your teenager's self-esteem may seem to totter precariously from day to day. Peer pressure is now at its peak. Why not sit down and write out all you can remember about the teenage years. You'll probably remember that the right clothes, the right hairstyle, the right friends, and even the right neighborhood can seemingly make or break a teenager's acceptance by his peers. Furthermore, it can be a particularly bad time if his parents decide to move, get a divorce, or suffer a financial downfall. And yet these things do happen, and teenagers survive even when they're sure they won't. We can make these difficult years easier for our child by realizing that he's still the exciting creation he was at birth. Consider these suggestions.

1. Allow your teenager to wear a reasonably popular mode of dress and hairstyle. Chances are, he'll return to the excellent taste you've taught him—later on.
2. If your teenager seems friendless, help him discover a group he can belong to. He might find one through the church, an after-school club at the Y.M.C.A., or special lessons at the community center. Really brainstorm here—development of skills continues to be important.
3. Make home a warm, safe haven—not a house of wrath and constant punishment. Continue to express love verbally.
4. Show an interest in what your teenager is doing, remembering to listen and ask questions.
5. If your teenager is suffering more than the normal pains of adolescence, and you realize you've never helped build his self-esteem in the early years, follow the steps under "Reconstructing Self-esteem" (further along in this chapter). You can help him enter the world a whole, fully equipped person.

But learning how to *react* to our children is only half of the picture. Our children can grow strong or weak under the influence of our own self-esteem bank.

When a friend telephoned to tell me that her daughters would not be able to play with Heather because they were going to bed early, Heather reacted with self-doubt.

"The truth is," she said, "Mrs. Jones just doesn't want me to play with her girls."

I laughed at the ridiculousness of the statement and then stopped abruptly with realization. It had been a bad week for me professionally. At least three manuscripts I had tried to publish had found their way back to my mailbox, and I had verbally announced that no one wanted my writing. Heather was merely reacting to life as her role model had done earlier.

No one can feel self-worth all the time, but knowing that

we're always acceptable to Christ can help us sincerely and
enthusiastically work toward the development of self-esteem.

RECONSTRUCTING SELF-ESTEEM

Karl Albrecht has written some excellent advice on rebuilding
one's self-esteem in his book, *Executive Tune-up: Personal
Effectiveness Skills for Business and Professional People.* He
tells us that regardless of where we are on the self-esteem
ladder, we all began forming our self-image very early in life.
Some of us developed a positive self-esteem as a result of
supportive childhood experiences, while others developed a
negative self-esteem as a result of discouraging experiences.
It doesn't really matter who was responsible for handing out
these messages—*we* bear the responsibility for retaining
these negative images. If we truly want the inner strength
that comes with owning a strong, positive self-image, we can
revise our present low self-esteem and the behavior that
accompanies it.

Start today by following these steps.

1. Strive to make yourself a likable person. To hold someone
    in high esteem usually implies we feel a personal sense
    of attraction to that person . . . that we like him. Think of
    yourself as that other person and begin by learning to like
    yourself. Minimize traits which in other people turn you
    off (those who are rude, irritable, complaining, opinion-
    ated, dull, etc.). If these things can discourage you from
    liking someone, imagine the harm they can do to your
    self-image. By adopting certain behaviors associated with
    a higher self-esteem, however, you can rise to the level of
    respect you desire.

    In *Positive Imaging*, author Norman Vincent Peale
    suggests studying oneself in the mirror. What kind of
    expression do you usually wear? Is it a smile or a frown?
    Are you usually cheerful or do you project an aura of
    depression? Do you have straight, energetic posture or do
    you slump in dejection? Are you attractively groomed
    or do you expect people to accept you in any condition?
    We probably won't ever be free of all our negative traits,

1. but reducing these problems will help us respect ourselves, and other people will hold us in higher esteem.
2. Eliminate self-condemning or negative statements about yourself. Don't describe yourself as dumb, crazy, fat, no good, etc. Accept compliments without adding a self-defeating remark.
3. Take credit for your strengths and accomplishments—recognize any improvement in your self-esteem and be proud.
4. Practice what you do well and gain confidence from a successful performance. Whether it's for baking a cake or writing computer programs, the praise you receive for a job well done will build self-esteem.
5. Toss out the "I can'ts." Make a list of the things you'd like to do but always believed you couldn't. (Examples: ballet dancing, horseback riding, entertaining.) Start with one item and make plans to achieve your goal. You may need lessons—but you might be procrastinating out of fear. One by one, reduce your list.
6. Refuse to accept put-downs. Let unfavorable remarks bounce off you by ignoring them. You can also change the subject or ask that the statement be repeated. In the last instance, the responsible person will probably be so embarrassed, he'll never again subject you to a put-down.

So today, I'm going to make a renewed effort toward polishing my own self-esteem. I will:

■ Realize even great people suffer moments of insecurity. (Read Exodus 4.)
■ Remember that no matter how many rejections I receive during the day, I am chosen by God.

But you are a chosen people, a royal priesthood, a holy nation, a people belonging to God . . . (1 Peter 2:9, NIV).

I am going to accept God's love. And do you know what? I have the strangest feeling that my security will shine forth in Heather like the sun itself.

Give your self-esteem an annual checkup by completing the following form.

CONFIDENTIAL/ANNUAL REPORT

Name _____ , Inc. (your name)

Assets:

Age _____   Talents _____
                                 _____
                                 _____

Hobbies _____   Skills _____
        _____   _____
        _____   _____

Life experiences _____   Financial status _____
                 _____
                 _____

Education _____   Health _____
          _____
          _____

Greatest ambitions _____   Good ideas _____
                   _____   _____
                   _____   _____

Other _____

Liabilities:

Age _____   Bad habits _____

Illnesses _____   Financial status _____

_____

Lack of motivation _____

Education needed _____

Other _____

Future Plans:
(Describe each)

To travel _____

_____

To own a business _____

_____

To go to college _____

_____

To develop a talent _____

_____

To get more exercise _____

_____

Other _____

_____

This report is a true and accurate accounting of the above-named corporation which is certified to be in:

Excellent _____

Good _____

Poor _____ condition.

C.P.A.

_____

HAVING IT ALL

As I come to the end of this book, a second child kicks impatiently within my womb, and I am once again excited with the knowledge that motherhood is always a woman's highest calling. And yet, this time there is a difference in how I perceive my role as a mother.

It's weeks away from the date of birth, but already, my child care is arranged, and my plans for returning to the typewriter are set. For I am not the full-time homemaker of Heather's infancy. . . . I am a working mother . . . content, fulfilled, and still looking to King Lemuel's ideal of the virtuous woman:

A wife of noble character who can find?
She is worth far more than rubies.
Her husband has full confidence in her and lacks nothing of
    value.
She brings him good, not harm, all the days of her life.
She selects wool and flax and works with eager hands.
She is like the merchant ships, bringing her food from afar.
She gets up while it is still dark; she provides food for her
    family and portions for her servant girls.
She considers a field and buys it; out of her earnings she
    plants a vineyard.
She sets about her work vigorously; her arms are strong for
    her tasks.
She sees that her trading is profitable, and her lamp does not
    go out at night.
In her hand she holds the distaff and grasps the spindle with
    her fingers.
She opens her arms to the poor and extends her hands to the
    needy.
When it snows, she has no fear for her household; for all of
    them are clothed in scarlet.
She makes coverings for her bed; she is clothed in fine linen
    and purple.
Her husband is respected at the city gate, where he takes his
    seat among the elders of the land.
She makes linen garments and sells them, and supplies the
    merchants with sashes.

She is clothed with strength and dignity; she can laugh at the
days to come.
She speaks with wisdom, and faithful instruction is on her
tongue.
She watches over the affairs of her household and does not
eat the bread of idleness.
Her children arise and call her blessed; her husband also,
and he praises her:
"Many women do noble things, but you surpass them all."
Charm is deceptive, and beauty is fleeting; but a woman who
fears the Lord is to be praised.
Give her the reward she has earned, and let her works bring
her praise at the city gate (Proverbs 31:10-31, NIV).

Yes, women have come a long way through the years. Not
on our own, as popular cliches would have us believe, but
by the power and grace of our Lord Jesus Christ. Finally, we
are taking the rightful position intended for us. And while
stepping into the combined role of wage earner and family
caretaker will always seem a gargantuan challenge, we know
it will never be more than we can handle or less than our
hearts desire—because God loves us.

And so today, I say:

"Thank you, Lord, for making me a woman . . . for making
me whole. I love you, too.

"Amen."

BIBLIOGRAPHY

BOOKS

Albrecht, Karl. *Executive Tune-up*. Englewood Cliffs, N.J.: Prentice-Hall, 1981.

Boston Women's Health Book Collective. *The New Our Bodies, Ourselves*. New York: Simon & Schuster, 1985.

Coffey, Barbara. *Glamour's Success Book*. New York: Simon & Schuster, 1983.

Curran, Dolores. *Traits of a Healthy Family*. Minneapolis: Winston Press, 1983.

David, Jay. *How to Play the Moonlighting Game*. New York: Facts on File, 1983.

Fanning, Robbie, and Tony Fanning. *Get It All Done and Still Be Human*. Radnor, Penn.: Chilton, 1979.

Good Housekeeping. *101 Practical Ways to Make Money at Home*. New York: Good Housekeeping, 1971.

Home and School Institute. *Families Learning Together*. New York: Simon & Schuster, 1981.

Insel, Paul M., and Walton T. Roth. *Core Concepts in Health*. Palo Alto, Calif.: Mayfield, 1979.

Long, Lynette, and Thomas Long. *The Handbook for Latchkey Children and Their Parents*. New York: Arbor House, 1983.

Melton, David. *Survival Kit for Parents of Teenagers*. New York: St. Martin's, 1979.

Miller, Maureen. *Help Your Child for Life*. Niles, Ill.: Argus, 1978.

Novello, Joseph R. *Bringing Up Kids American Style*. New York: A & W, 1981.

Peale, Norman Vincent. *Positive Imaging*. Old Tappan, N.J.: Revell, 1981.

Pinkham, Mary Ellen. *Mary Ellen's Best of Helpful Hints, Book Two*. New York: Warner, 1981.

Posner, Mitchell. *Executive Essentials*. New York: Avon, 1982.

Rinella, Richard J., and Clair C. Robbins. *Career Power*. New York: American Management Association, 1980.

Ryglewicz, Hilary, and Pat Koch Thaler. *Working Couples*. New York: Simon & Schuster, 1980.

Satir, Virginia M. *Peoplemaking*. Palo Alto, Calif.: Science and Behavior, 1972.

Urieli, Nachman, and Vivienne Sernaque. *Part-Time Jobs*. New York: Ballantine, 1982.

Wallach, Janet. *Working Wardrobe*. Washington, D.C.: Acropolis, 1981.

Witt, Scott. *Second Income Money Makers*. West Nyack, N.Y.: Parker, 1975.

NEWSPAPERS

Johnson, Janis. "Should Parents Be Tough or Easy?" *USA Today,* June 25, 1985.

Jurgens, Gay. "Couples Keep Excitement Alive." *Dallas Morning News,* June 23, 1985.

Peterson, Karen S. "The Price of Succeeding Too Soon." *USA Today,* June 11, 1985.

PERIODICALS

Brinley, Maryann. "Reassuring Answers to 10 Myths about Day Care." *McCall's,* January 1985.

Jacoby, Susan. "I'd Like a Better Job, But I'm Stuck." *McCall's,* July 1985.

Nelson, Debra, and James Quick. "Professional Women: Are Distress and Disease Inevitable?" *Academy of Management Review,* April 1985.

Sleeter, Michael. "Keep 'Em Laughing." *Working Woman,* October 1981.

INDEX